U0829574

美丽扬州

BEAUTIFUL YANGZHOU

（汉英对照）

主　　编：辜伟节

副 主 编：朱雪梅　张利琴

中文作者：朱雪梅　刘广其　茅娉婷

英文译者：张利琴　王　燕　范洪亚　刘　娟　张　瑾　孙　涛

英文审校：Vera Okhlyakovskaya　Megan Cramer　Kimberly Cramer

译林出版社

图书在版编目（CIP）数据

美丽扬州：汉英对照／辜伟节，朱雪梅，张利琴主编．—南京：译林出版社，2012.8（2024.7重印）
ISBN 978-7-5447-2807-2

Ⅰ.①美… Ⅱ.①辜…②朱…③张… Ⅲ.①扬州市－概况－汉、英 Ⅳ.①K925.33

中国版本图书馆 CIP 数据核字（2012）第 088390 号

美丽扬州（汉英对照）

责任编辑 李浩瑜 鲍迎迎
责任印制 董 虎

出版发行 译林出版社
地 址 南京市湖南路 1 号 A 楼
邮 箱 jiaocai@yilin.com
网 址 www.yilin.com, edu.yilin.com
编辑热线 025-83658349, 83672889
排 版 南京展望文化发展有限公司
印 刷 江苏凤凰扬州鑫华印刷有限公司
开 本 652 毫米 × 960 毫米 1/16
印 张 11.75
版 次 2012 年 8 月第 1 版
印 次 2024 年 7 月第 19 次印刷
书 号 ISBN 978-7-5447-2807-2
定 价 22.00 元

版权所有 · 侵权必究
译林版图书若有印装错误可向出版社调换。 质量热线：025-83658316

前　言

扬州，一座位于江苏中部、长江北岸的历史文化名城，无论是其秀美的自然风光、独特的园林古迹，亦或是其璀璨的文化艺术、精致的美味佳肴，都闪耀着可观、可察、可品的古都之美。

为了让更多的人了解扬州之美，让扬州人增添更多的爱乡之情，我们编写了《美丽扬州》（汉英对照）这本书。限于篇幅，本书只撷取了扬州之美的少量代表加以呈现，并尽量以图文并茂的方式诠释扬州的美丽与精致。现今，扬州是一座捷步走向世界的开放城市，学会用英文介绍扬州之美，已经成为时代的需求，这也正是我们进行双语写作的主旨。鉴于此，本书既可作为扬州市中学生的地方课程读物与英语拓展读物，也可作为扬州旅游管理专业学生的双语导游词，还可作为向广大旅游爱好者、国际友人介绍扬州风情的读本。

本书由扬州市教育局领导提出策划方案，由辜伟节、朱雪梅确定编写框架，全书中文稿由朱雪梅统稿，辜伟节审稿。各章中文稿编写分工如下：第一章、第三章由刘广其编写，第二章、第六章由朱雪梅编写，第四章、第五章由茅娉婷编写。全书英文翻译由张利琴统稿、校译，各章译者如下：第一章由范洪亚翻译，第二章由张利琴、张瑾翻译，第三章由王燕翻译，第四章由刘娟翻译，第五章由张利琴、孙涛翻译，第六章由张利琴翻译。

本书得以出版发行，是集体智慧的结晶。首先感谢扬州市人民政府、扬州市旅游局、扬州市申遗办、广陵书社等单位的大力支持，他们提供了许多宝贵的资料。特别感谢韦明铧先生给予的无私帮助，他不仅从扬州文化研究的专业视角审阅了全书，而且解答了编者的许多疑惑和难题。特别感谢本书的责任编辑叶宁庆先生、鲍迎迎女士以犀利的目光找出了书稿中的误点，感谢他们为本书的出版付出的艰辛劳动。另外，在本书的编写过程中，有部分资料与图片因种种原因未能找到作者，请作者见书后与我们联系，以便奉上稿酬。

由于编者才疏学浅，虽然竭尽全力，但错误难免，敬请广大读者批评指正。

目 录

Contents

第一章
扬州印象

扬州历史悠久，是国务院公布的首批24座历史文化名城之一。到2014年，扬州将迎来她的2500华诞。扬州也是首批“中国优秀旅游城市”、“国家环保模范城市”、“国家园林城市”，扬州市政府曾获得“联合国人居奖”这一殊荣。作为“淮左名都”，扬州古迹众多，园林秀丽，物产丰饶。

西汉早期，扬州第一次走向繁荣。隋炀帝开通大运河以后，隋唐时期的扬州是全国商业最繁华的都会。清代，扬州再次成为全国著名的商业城市，这主要得益于其位于大运河与长江交汇处。长江流域广大地区以及许多来自海外的物资和人员北上，多需经过扬州，优越的地理位置，使其成为重要的交通与商业中心。

扬州周边地区属于平原水乡，气候温暖湿润，东靠盛产海盐的黄海，物产丰富，为商业贸易的繁荣提供了丰厚的物质基础。

Chapter I

Impressions on Yangzhou

Owing to its long history, Yangzhou is among the first 24 cities in China that enjoy the title of Historical and Cultural City approved by the State Council. By the year 2014, Yangzhou will mark its 2,500th anniversary of the founding of the city. In the recent years, the city was among the first to win the titles of Top Tourist City of China, National Model City in Environmental Protection, National-level Garden City, and Habitat Scroll of Honor Award by the United Nations. As A Famous City East of the Huai River, Yangzhou boasts quite a few historical sites, beautiful scenic gardens and abundant local products.

As early as the beginning of the Western Han Dynasty, the first signs of prosperity appeared in Yangzhou. With the completion of the Grand Canal during the reign of Emperor Yang in the Sui Dynasty, Yangzhou became the biggest metropolitan area nationwide. In the Qing Dynasty, Yangzhou once again became a famous commercial center due to its favored location at the confluence of the Grand Canal and the Yangtze River, which provided easy access to the north from most areas around the Yangtze River and even abroad, and thus guaranteed its importance as a significant transportation and commercial center.

Close to the seasalt-rich Yellow Sea in the east, Yangzhou belongs to the humid subtropical climate zone, giving it a temperate climate. It is a flatland webbed with rivers and lakes and is rich in natural resources. All of these factors contribute to the city's commercial prosperity.

第一节　悠久的历史

扬州的土地上很早就有人类居住。20世纪90年代，在今天高邮市区东北约10公里的龙虬庄遗址，出土了两千余件石器、玉器、骨角器、陶器等生产、生活用具以及几千粒炭化稻谷。这些距今7000—5500年前的文化遗物证明，江淮地区和长江流域、黄河流域一样，同为中华文明的发源地。

春秋—魏晋

扬州有近2500年的历史。西周时期，现在的扬州市区附近有一个邗国。到了春秋初期，江南的吴国兼并了邗国，逐步将势力往北扩展到淮河边。公元前486年，为了北上伐齐，与晋国争霸，吴王夫差修建了连接长江与淮河的邗沟，以利于运粮运兵和舟师的快速进退，并在邗沟与长江的交汇处（今市区西北郊蜀岗一带）修筑邗城。这就是目前已知的最初的扬州城。

· 古邗沟

扬州市区邗沟路南侧的河道便是古邗沟遗址。古邗沟由螺丝湾桥下往西不远，便转弯向北，在到达北边的土岗脚下后再转向西，经过今保障湖，一直到观音山脚下。邗沟的开凿，方便了南北交通，为后来扬州经济文化的发展创造了条件。

不久，越灭吴，扬州属越。之后越又为楚所灭，扬州属楚。楚国在邗城旧址上建广陵城，扬州称广陵由此开始。

Section One A Long History

Some of the earliest traces of Chinese inhabitants are found on the land of Yangzhou. In the 1990s, in ancient relics of the Longqiu village—roughly 10 kilometers northeast of modern-day Gaoyou city, more than two thousand pieces of ancient working tools and utensils like stoneware, jadeware, hornware, pottery, as well as several thousand grains of carbonized rice were unearthed. These 5500-to-7000-year-old artifacts clearly prove that the Jianghuai basin (the area between the Yangtze River and the Huai River), the Yangtze River basin and the Yellow River basin are the cradle lands of Chinese civilization.

From the Spring and Autumn Period to the Wei and Jin Dynasties

Yangzhou has a history of nearly 2,500 years. During the Western Zhou Dynasty, there used to be the Han State next to the present-day urban areas of Yangzhou. Later, at the beginning of the Spring and Autumn Period, the Han State merged into the Wu State to the south of the Yangtze River, which gradually expanded to the north of the Huai River. In 486 BC, in order to conquer the Qi State in the north and compete for supremacy with the Jin State, Fuchai, King of the State of Wu, had the Han Canal built, which connected the Yangtze River and the Huai River, thus providing a convenient route for transporting troops and food supplies, as well as allowing the navy to advance and retreat quickly. He also built the Hancheng where the Yangtze River and the Han Canal met, over the the Shugang Ridge to the northwest of present-day Yangzhou. The Hancheng was the precursor of the urban area of Yangzhou.

The river to the south of the present-day Han Canal Road of Yangzhou city originated from the ancient Han Canal, flowing west under the Luosiwan Bridge, turning north in the near distance, reaching the north foot of the hill before turning west, and then running through the present-day Baozhang Lake to the foot of the Guanyin Mountain. The construction of the Han Canal provided convenient transportation between the North and the South, and later created favorable conditions for economic and cultural development of Yangzhou.

Shortly after, the Yue State conquered the Wu State, and Yangzhou became part of the Yue State. Afterwards, Yangzhou became part of the Chu State after Yue was under the control of Chu. Chu constructed the city of Guangling on the site of the Hancheng, thus making Guangling the precursor of the present-day Yangzhou.

两汉时期，扬州长期是藩王的封地，先后建立过荆国、吴国、江都国、广陵国。刘邦平定淮南王英布的叛乱后，封侄子刘濞为吴王。刘濞在吴国境内大力发展农业、冶铁业、造船业，并且开采铜矿，炼铜铸钱。同时，他又开凿了由茱萸湾向东经泰州到海滨的运盐河（通扬运河的前身），将海边生产的海盐运往广陵销售，赚取了大量的钱财，使吴国成为西汉经济实力最强的藩国，这也是扬州历史上的第一次繁荣时期。后来刘濞联合其他六国，起兵造反，掀起历史上著名的“七国之乱”，想夺取中央政权，最终兵败被杀。事后，汉景帝改吴国为江都国，将自己的儿子刘非封为江都王，由贤人董仲舒辅佐。

· 隋炀帝

魏晋南北朝时期是国家大分裂、民族大融合的时期，也是江南经济大发展的时期。扬州作为江淮军事重镇，在那样一个战乱频繁的时代，屡次繁荣，又屡遭浩劫。

隋唐—宋元

公元589年，隋文帝统一中国，设扬州总管府，广陵始称扬州。隋炀帝在邗沟的基础上开通了南北大运河，使扬州成为“南北舟车之会”，为唐代扬州的极度繁荣奠定了基础。运河开通后，隋炀帝曾三下扬州，在这里居住停留的时间累计达三年两个月之久，最终被其禁卫军首领缢死在扬州。

During the Western and Eastern Han Dynasties, Yangzhou had successively been under control of the seigniors from the Jing State, the Wu State, the Jiangdu State and the Guangling State. After suppressing the rebellion of Ying Bu (King of the Huainan State), King Liu Bang in the Han Dynasty made Liu Bi, a nephew of his, King of the State of Wu. In his territory, Liu Bi started developing agriculture, metallurgical industry, shipbuilding industry, and copper mining for mint. Meanwhile, he made a river (predecessor of the Nantong-Yangzhou Canal) dug from the Mastixia Bay (known as Zhuyuwan) all the way east through Taizhou to the coast, specially used for transporting the seasalt to Guangling for sale. In this way, the State of Wu became the most economically powerful state in the Western Han Dynasty. Hence, the first signs of economic prosperity appeared in the history of Yangzhou. Later Liu Bi initiated the Rebellion of the Seven States, during which he was defeated and killed. Afterwards, Emperor Jing of the Han Dynasty renamed the State of Wu as the State of Jiangdu, and made his son Liu Fei the King of Jiangdu, who was assisted by a wise scholar Dong Zhongshu.

The Wei and Jin Dynasties and Southern and Northern Dynasties was a period when the country faced division and unification of all nations. It was also a period of economic boom in the south of the Yangtze River. In such a time full of unrest and wars, Yangzhou, experienced dramatic ups and downs as a city of military importance.

From the Sui and Tang Dynasties to the Song and Yuan Dynasties

In 589 AD, Emperor Wen of the Sui Dynasty unified China. Following the establishment of Zongguanfu (a local administrative government center equivalent to a present-day prefecture-level city), Guangling was officially renamed Yangzhou. Based on the Han Canal, Emperor Yang of the Sui Dynasty started the construction of the Grand Canal to connect the North and the South, making Yangzhou "a transportation hub city", which laid a solid foundation for its later prosperity in the Tang Dynasty. After the completion of the Grand Canal, Emperor Yang paid three visits to Yangzhou. All his stays in Yangzhou added up to a total of three years and two months. With Northern China in turmoil, Emperor Yang spent his last days in Jiangdu (present-day Yangzhou), where he was eventually strangled by his general.

隋朝以后，我国的政治中心虽在北方，但经济来源却倚靠南方。得天独厚的地理位置，使得扬州在唐朝时期达到了历史上的鼎盛。长江流域广大地区的粮食、物资和人员北上，多需要经过扬州。当时，扬州经济繁荣，商贾云集，文化发达，成为仅次于长安、洛阳的全国第三大城市，也是中国四大商港之一和海上丝绸之路的重要起点之一，其商业繁华程度居全国第一。公元753年，享誉全国的高僧、扬州大明寺住持鉴真和尚应日本遣唐使的邀请远赴日本，将大唐丰富的文化传播到日本。

· 扬州宋大城西门遗址

宋朝时期，扬州分别属淮南道、淮南路、淮南东路，元朝时属扬州路。北宋时期，扬州仍是中国东南地区的经济、文化中心，商业税收在全国居第三位。两宋时期，欧阳修、苏东坡出任扬州太守；韩世忠、刘锜、岳飞在扬州附近抗击金兵；南宋时期，伊斯兰教创始人穆罕默德十六世孙普哈丁在扬州传教；元朝时期，马可•波罗在扬州任职三年。

明清—当代

明朝时期，扬州称淮海府、维扬府、扬州府。清朝亦称扬州府。

· 清代扬州两淮盐运使司衙署

清代，扬州繁华以盐盛。清代中期，扬州居交通要冲，是我国中部各省食盐的供应基地和南北漕运的咽喉要塞。随着商品经济特别是盐业的发展，扬州再次成为全国著名的商业城市，也是当时世界上人口超过50万的十大城市之一。清政府的盐税与财政收入关系很大，当时扬州盐税占全国盐税的五分之三。

After the Sui Dynasty, with its political center in the North, the country relied mainly on the South for economic resources. In the Tang Dynasty, Yangzhou reached its peak prosperity because it was then a distribution center of food supplies, commercial goods, and laborers. Prosperity also attracted countless officials, merchants, poets, and artists. Therefore, Yangzhou became the third largest city in the country, closely after Chang'an and Luoyang. It was also one of China's four largest ports, and the starting point of the Maritime Silk Road, ranking first in business. In 753 AD, at the invitation of the Japanese diplomats, a nationally renowned monk, Jian Zhen from Yangzhou Daming Temple, went to Japan, bringing rich Tang culture.

During the Song Dynasty, Yangzhou was under the administration of Huainan Dao (a local administrative government center equivalent to present-day prefecture-level city), later called Huainan Lu, East Huainan Lu, and finally Yangzhou Lu in the Yuan Dynasty. In the Northern Song Dynasty, Yangzhou remained the economic and cultural center of China's southeast region, with its business taxes ranking the third throughout the country. During the Song Dynasty, Ou Yangxiu and Su Dongpo acted as prefect of Yangzhou; Han Shizhong, Liu Qi, and Yue Fei led armies fighting against the invaders from the kingdom of Jin to the vicinity of Yangzhou; Puhaddin, the sixteenth descendant of Mohamed—the founder of the Islam, came here to do missionary work in the Southern Song Dynasty; Marco Polo, an Italian traveler, held a post in Yangzhou for three years in the Yuan Dynasty.

From the Ming and Qing Dynasties to the Present

During the Ming Dynasty, Yangzhou was renamed Huaihai Fu (superior prefecture), later Weiyang Fu, and finally Yangzhou Fu. In the Qing Dynasty, the present-day Yangzhou city was also named Yangzhou Fu.

During the Qing Dynasty, Yangzhou salt industry was flourishing. In the middle of the Qing Dynasty, Yangzhou, a gateway city, was a salt supply base for central provinces of our country and the North-South water transport throat (It refers to the transport of grain by water to the capital or for military supplies in ancient times) for the Qing government. With the development of its commodity economy, especially the development of salt industry, Yangzhou once again became a rich region with unparalleled commercial prosperity, as well as one of the ten biggest cities in the world with a population over 500,000. At that time, salt tax was an important source of the revenue of the Qing government,

清朝初年即在扬州设立两淮巡盐御史和淮南盐运司，曹雪芹的祖父曹寅就曾担任两淮巡盐御史。康熙和乾隆都曾六下江南，两位皇帝共十一次视察扬州。康熙南巡，多以扬州为中心，致力于治理“黄患”（当时黄河经淮安向东入海），疏通运河，整修港埠，使运河动脉畅通。

在文化艺术方面，以郑板桥为代表的扬州画派、以阮元为代表的扬州学派使得扬州文化在全国独领风骚。

十九世纪以后，由于国家食盐销售制度的改革、京杭运河山东段的淤塞、太平天国运动中战争的破坏以及近代铁路、海运的兴起等原因，扬州经济萧条，民不聊生。

新中国成立后，扬州这片土地重现勃勃生机。目前，扬州立足于“创新扬州、精致扬州、幸福扬州”这一目标，努力建设为古代文化与现代文明交相辉映的名城。

accounting for three fifths of the national tax. North-South Huai River Salt Censorship Office and Southern Huai River Salt Transportation Division were established in Yangzhou in the early years of the Qing Dynasty, both in the charge of appointed officials. Cao Yin, grandfather of the famous writer Cao Xueqin, was once the inspector in the North-South Huai River Salt Censorship Office. Emperors Kangxi and Qianlong paid a total of eleven visits to Yangzhou during their respective six tours to the south of the Yangtze River. During his southern inspection tours, Emperor Kangxi mainly focused on Yangzhou, devoting himself to the control of the Yellow River floods (the Yellow River ran into the East Sea via Huai'an area at that time), dredging the Grand Canal, and renovating ports and to make the Grand Canal a smooth transportation artery.

At the time, the Yangzhou School of Painting with Zheng Banqiao as the main representative, and the Yangzhou School of Thought with Ruan Yuan as the main representative, secured Yangzhou a position of great significance in Chinese culture.

After the nineteenth century, due to the national reform of salt sales system, the blockage of Beijing-Hangzhou Canal in Shandong Province, the devastation caused by the Taiping Heavenly Kingdom Movement and the rise of modern railway, shipping, and many other reasons, Yangzhou was faced with economic downturns. Its people suffered terribly.

Since the foundation of the People's Republic of China, Yangzhou has been full of vitality again. At present, with the goal of building an "innovative Yangzhou, exquisite Yangzhou, happy Yangzhou", Yangzhou is striving to build itself into a famous city where the ancient culture and the modern civilization reflect and complement each other magnificently.

第二节　优越的环境

扬州位于我国东部沿海地区，地处亚热带平原水乡。在古代，由于扬州位于大运河与长江交汇处，地理位置得天独厚，造就了它的几度繁荣。近现代时期，扬州处于我国经济发达的长江三角洲地区，受到上海等大城市的辐射，发展外向型经济的条件也较为优越。

概况

扬州是苏中地区重要的政治、经济、文化中心和交通枢纽。扬州位于江苏省中部、长江下游北岸，地处京杭运河与长江交汇处，滨江近海，地理位置十分优越。目前，扬州市管辖广陵区、邗江区、江都区和宝应县，并代管仪征市与高邮市。其范围大致在北纬32° 15′ ～33° 25′ 、东经119° 01′ ～119° 54′ 之间，全市总面积6634平方千米，人口465万（2011年），其中扬州城区人口约为229万。

气候

扬州处在亚热带的北部，气候温暖湿润，四季分明。年平均气温14.9℃。最冷的1月平均气温为1.8℃，最热的7月平均气温为27.6℃。多年年平均降水量为1030毫米，降水主要集中在5月到9月。梅雨季节大致在每年的6月中旬开始，7月中旬结束，降水量约占全年的25%。

· 扬州之春

· 扬州之秋

“烟花三月下扬州”道出了诗仙李白对春日扬州的无限向往。扬州春

Section Two Predominant Ecological Environment

Yangzhou is located in the region of rivers and lakes in the subtropical plains along the eastern coastline of China. In ancient times, due to its perfect geographic location—lying in the confluence of the Grand Canal and the Yangtze River, Yangzhou witnessed quite a few dynasties of prosperity. In modern times, as it lies in the country's most economically-developed Yangtze River Delta and within the scope of economic influence of Shanghai and other big cities, Yangzhou enjoys quite favorable conditions for developing an export-oriented economy.

General Information

In addition to being the political, economic and cultural center in central Jiangsu Province, Yangzhou is the transportation hub within the region. Due to its location on the north bank of lower Yangtze River in central Jiangsu Province, at the confluence of the Grand Canal and the Yangtze River, off the coast of the Yellow Sea, Yangzhou enjoys an extremely advantageous geographic location. As a prefecture-level city, Yangzhou city jurisdiction includes 6 county-level divisions: Baoying County, two county-level cities (Yizheng and Gaoyou) and three districts, namely Guangling, Hanjiang and Jiangdu. It is located at 119°01′-119°54′ east longitude and 32°15′-33°25′ north latitude. The city covers a total area of 6,634 square kilometers with a population of 4,650,000 (according to the census in 2011), among which the urban population is about 2,290,000.

Climate

Yangzhou is located in the north humid subtropical climate zone with four clearly defined seasons and temperate climate. Its annual average temperature is 14.9°C. The coldest month is January, with an average temperature of 1.8°C. The hottest month is July, with an average temperature of 27.6°C. For many years, the average yearly rainfall has stayed at about 1,030 mm, mostly from May to September. The rainy season, known as Plum Rain Season, usually lasts from mid-June to mid-July, accounting for about 25% of whole year's rainfall.

In the poem "Take a journey to Yangzhou in the misty flowery March" by Li Bai, a famous poet in the Tang Dynasty, he fully expressed his yearning for springtime of Yangzhou. Spring in Yangzhou lasts from

季始于三月下旬，终于五月底。农历三月是扬州一年中最为迷人的时节。此时，桃李争艳，杨柳堆烟，百鸟争鸣，春意盎然。

秋季自九月中旬起至十一月中旬结束。这期间，天高云淡，阳光灿烂，秋风送爽，天气稳定少变。

地形

· 平原风光

扬州市地形以平原为主，仅在仪征和邗江的北部分布着坡度和缓、岗顶宽平的丘陵。平原以新通扬运河为界，运河以北属江淮平原，以南属长江三角洲。

江淮平原在扬州市境内又以大运河为界，分为东、西两部分，西部为运西湖区平原，东部为里下河平原。扬州市境内绝大部分地方地势低平、河湖密布，是著名的水乡。

扬州市西南部的丘陵海拔多在30—50米之间，其中仪征大铜山海拔149米，为全市最高点。也正因为这一带广泛覆盖着丘陵，战国时期的扬州才被称为“广陵”。许多丘陵表面覆盖着黄土，所以被称为“黄土岗地”，如城西北著名的蜀岗风景区就是一片黄土岗地。

扬州的丘陵地区分布有若干茶场和水库，仪征捺山茶场、月塘登月湖，是市民乡村游和自驾游的好去处。市区甘泉山、高邮神居山、仪征庙山这些地势高爽的丘陵，成为汉代扬州郡王墓葬的首选之地。

late March to the end of May. The best time to visit Yangzhou is the third month in the Chinese lunar calendar, when peaches and plums are in full blossom, birds sing to each other, and willow trees are coated with blooms in the mist.

Autumn lasts from mid-September till mid-November. During this period, the sky appears higher and clouds lighter. The weather stays cool and clear with bright sunshine.

Topography

Yangzhou is located mainly on flatland. It only has hilly land with gentle slopes and wide and flat tops in Yizheng and northern Hanjiang. The plain lies on both sides of the new Nantong-Yangzhou Canal, to the north of which belongs to the Jianghuai Plain and to the south of which belongs to the Yangtze River Delta.

The Jianghuai Plain in Yangzhou city lies on both sides of the Grand Canal, with the riverside areas to the east of the Grand Canal and plains to the west. Most of the land in Yangzhou is low and flat terrain densely webbed by rivers and lakes, giving it the name of "a land of rivers and lakes".

Hills in southwest of Yangzhou city are mostly at an elevation from 30 to 50 meters, among which Datong Hill in Yizheng, the highest point of Yangzhou city, reaches 149 meters above sea level. In the Warring States Period, Yangzhou was named Guangling mainly because it is covered with a wide range of low hills. Many hilly areas are coated with loess, hence the name "loess highland". The scenic spot of the Shugang Ridge to the northwest of the present-day Yangzhou is a loess highland area.

The Yangzhou hilly area is dotted with tea plantations and reservoirs. Nashan tea plantation in Yizheng and Dengyue (Mounting Moon) Lake in Yuetang town of Yizheng are favorite places for city residents to visit. Historically, relatively higher and cooler hills like Ganquan Mountain in the urban areas, Shenju (God Dwelling) Mountain in Gaoyou, and Temple Mountain in Yizheng used to be the first choices for tombs for Yangzhou seigniors in the Han Dynasty.

·凤凰岛湿地

河湖湿地

扬州市水域面积共2000多平方千米，约占全市总面积的30%。运西湖区平原上，大中型湖泊成群，烟波浩渺，水天一色。里下河平原上河汊密如蛛网，湖荡星罗棋布。市域南侧的长江江阔水深，受海潮影响，江水每天时涨时落。扬州自古以来就是一座秀水环绕的城市，市区河流纵横，桥梁座座，形态各异，构成了美丽的城市风光。

江都水利枢纽工程是亚洲最大的电力排灌工程，它使里下河平原成了遇旱能灌、遇涝能排、稳产高产的大粮仓。这里先后接待过许多中外贵宾和多国元首。现在，它又成为我国南水北调东线工程的源头。江都水利枢纽旅游区是国家级水利旅游风景区，区内建有多个景点，绿荫浓密，景色宜人，恰似一幅美丽画卷。

交通

扬州位于长三角经济圈，交通十分便利，公路、铁路、水路、航空等运输方式相互联通，形成了一个立体运输网络，为促进扬州经济的发展与对外交流提供了理想的条件。

目前，扬州市高速公路已形成以扬州市区为中心的“一环五射”高速路网，这个高速路网由宁通高速、京沪高速、沪陕高速和扬溧高速共同组成。现在从扬州坐汽车到上海虹桥机场只需两个半小时，到南京禄口国际机场只需一个多小时，到江都境内的扬州泰州机场则只需20分钟。

Rivers, Lakes and Wetlands

Waters in Yangzhou cover a total area of more than 2,000 square kilometers, which is about 30% of the whole area. On the plains to the west of the Grand Canal lie plenty of lakes of big and medium sizes, a vast expanse of misty waters reaching all the way to the horizon, reflecting the beautiful blue sky. The low plains between the Yangtze River and the Huai River are dotted with a cobweb of river branches and lakes. Running through the south of Yangzhou is the vast Yangtze River, whose water level rises and falls from time to time due to the influence of sea. Yangzhou has always been a beautiful city with water scenery surrounding its urban areas. Many rivers cross the landscape of the city with bridges of different shapes.

Jiangdu Water Conservancy Project is the largest electric irrigation and drainage engineering project in Asia, which ensures that the plains in low can reach an abundant and stable grain supply with timely irrigation during drought and timely drainage during floods. It has attracted a number of guests from home and abroad, including top leaders from different countries. Now, it has become the east source of China's South-to-North Water Diversion Project. Tourist areas in Jiangdu Water Conservancy Project offer picturesque lakeside views: perfect picnic spots in the shade of trees, pleasant scenery, and other attractions.

Traffic

Located in the Yangtze River Delta, Yangzhou enjoys a convenient three-dimensional transportation network that connects highways, railways, waterways and airlines, providing optimal conditions for fast economic development of Yangzhou as well as external communication.

At present, with the urban area of Yangzhou as its center, the "one ring and five directions" highway network has been formed, consisting of Nanjing-Nantong Expressway, Beijing-Shanghai Expressway, Shanghai-Shanxi Expressway and Yangzhou-Liyang Expressway. Now it takes only 2.5 hours to get to Shanghai Hongqiao Airport from Yangzhou Bus Station, a little more than an hour to Nanjing Lukou International Airport, and only 20 minutes to Yangzhou Taizhou Airport on the territory of Jiangdu.

宁启铁路穿过扬州，它是国家快速铁路网和长江三角洲地区城际轨道网的重要组成部分。该铁路目前正按国家Ⅰ级铁路标准进行复线电气化改造。到工程完工后，宁启铁路的通行时速将从目前的120公里提高到200公里。目前，每天有26个火车车次经停扬州火车站或从该站始发，分别开往北京、西安、成都、广州等城市。

经停扬州的主要列车车次简表	
车次	起止点
Z29/30次	扬州-北京
K414/5、K413/6次	扬州-青岛
K62/59、K60/61次	扬州-西安
K245/8、K247/6次	扬州-成都
K568/9、K567/570次	南通-重庆北
K384/1、K382/3次	南通-汉口
K432/4/1次	扬州-南昌
K224/1、K222/3次	泰州-广州
K94/1、K92/3次	泰州-深圳西

扬州泰州机场于2012年建成通航，拥有中型机场客流量。目前，已确定开通北京、广州、深圳、西安、厦门、沈阳、海口、成都、大连、昆明等多条国内航线，未来还有望开通日本、韩国和东南亚等国际航线。

扬州处在长江与京杭运河两大水运动脉的交汇地，内河运输非常发达。仪征市、江都区和扬州市区共有80.5千米长的长江岸线。京杭运河由北往南纵贯宝应、高邮和江都区，在境内全长143公里，是我国北煤南运的重要通道。

扬州港四号码头泊位

Important trains that stop at Yangzhou Station	
Train lines	Starting point–Destination
Z29/30	Yangzhou–Beijing
K414/5、K413/6	Yangzhou–Qingdao
K62/59、K60/61	Yangzhou–Xi'an
K245/8、K247/6	Yangzhou–Chengdu
K568/9、K567/570	Nantong–North Chongqing
K384/1、K382/3	Nantong–Hankou
K432/4/1	Yangzhou–Nanchang
K224/1、K222/3	Taizhou–Guangzhou
K94/1、K92/3	Taizhou–West Shenzhen

Nanjing-Qidong railway, a very important part of the national express railway network and inter-city rail network of the Yangtze River Delta, runs through Yangzhou. This railway is now under reconstruction in accordance with national first-class standards for multiple track electrification. Upon the completion of the project, the train will be accelerated from the current 120 kph to 200 kph. At present, 26 trains depart from or pass through Yangzhou every day, with destinations such as Beijing, Xi'an, Chengdu, Guangzhou, etc.

Yangzhou Taizhou Airport, which began operating in 2012, is a medium-sized airport. At present, it offers flights to domestic cities like Beijing, Guangzhou, Shenzhen, Xi'an, Xiamen, Shenyang, Haikou, Chengdu, Dalian, and Kunming. In the near future, the airport is expected to offer some international flights to Japan, Korea, Southeast Asia, etc.

Yangzhou enjoys a well-developed river transportation system due to its location right at the junction of the Yangtze River and Beijing-Hangzhou Grand Canal. It has 80.5 km of the Yangtze River riverbank, and two of its districts, Hanjiang and Jiangdu, as well as Yizheng city, are located along the river. Beijing-Hangzhou Grand Canal runs southward through Baoying, Gaoyou and Jiangdu, stretching for 143 kilometers in Yangzhou, and serves as a crucial waterway for shipping coal from the North to the South.

第三节 宜居的名城

自古以来，扬州既是文化名城，也是一些商人和文人雅士梦寐以求的栖居之地，成为一座以“宜居”闻名于世的城市。千百年来的居住习惯和理念，形成了富有扬州特色的人居文化。经过近些年的不懈努力，扬州获得了“国家卫生城市”、“国家园林城市”、“国家环保模范城市”、“联合国人居奖”等称号和荣誉，逐渐发展成为一座古代文化与现代文明相得益彰的宜居名城。

· 联合国人居奖纪念石刻

人生只合扬州死

扬州城建于春秋时期。到隋唐时，这里水陆交通四通八达，物产丰富，人杰地灵，是文人墨客和富商巨贾云集的地方。诗人杜牧的“十年一觉扬州梦”，写出了他徘徊流连、迟迟不舍离去的心情。与杜牧同时代的另一诗人张祜，则发出了“人生只合扬州死，禅智山光好墓田”的慨叹，指出扬州不仅是人间天堂，也是最好的人生归宿之处，体现了人们对扬州强烈的向往之情。

明代文人陈子龙送别友人时说“君去扬州便作家”，劝朋友在扬州砌宅造屋，创业安家。清代文人、《儒林外史》的作者吴敬梓，晚年经常在南京和扬州之间往还，并吟诵“人生只合扬州死”，后来真被他言中，在扬州与朋友的一次欢聚之后，他溘然而逝。

Section Three A Famous Paradise City

Known for its history and art, Yangzhou has always been world-famous for its residential environment and culture. It is an ideal dwelling place for both merchants and men of letters. Owing to its own living habits and ideas formed over thousands of years, the city has created rich residential tradition with unique local features. With untiring efforts through years, Yangzhou has won multiple awards, such as National-level Sanitary City, National-level Garden City, National Model City in Environmental Protection and Habitat Scroll of Honor Award by the United Nations. Thus it has gradually developed into a famous heavenly-habitat city with its ancient culture and modern civilization complementing each other magnificently.

Die and Be Buried in Yangzhou

As for the history of city building in Yangzhou, it can be traced as far back as the Spring and Autumn Period. By the time of the Sui and Tang Dynasties, Yangzhou, abundant in natural resources, had already been a thoroughfare for developed water system and land transportation routes as well as a gathering place for men of letters and rich businessmen. In a poem by Du Mu, "After ten years from a Yangzhou dream I woke", the poet's deep sentimental attachment to Yangzhou is vividly expressed. Poet Zhang Hu, a contemporary of Du Mu, heaved a sigh with such feeling, "What a pleasure to spend one's remaining years in Yangzhou, there is a chance that one can be buried in the picturesque mountain range where the Chanzhi Temple lies. " In his poem, Yangzhou is depicted as paradise on earth and an eternal heaven as well, reflecting people's intense longing for Yangzhou.

Chen Zilong, a scholar in the Ming Dynasty, wrote the poem "On your arrival in Yangzhou, better stay there" for his friend. He advised his friend to have his house built and then to settle down and start his business in Yangzhou. Wu Jingzi, a scholar in the Qing Dynasty and the author of *The Scholars*, spent his later years alternating between Nanjing and Yangzhou, chanting "Die and be buried in Yangzhou". Coincidently, after a happy gathering with his friends in Yangzhou, he passed away.

旧城人文古民居

改革开放以后，在新的历史时期，扬州给自己的城市定位是历史文化名城、具有传统特色的风景旅游城市、适宜人居的生态园林城市。如今，经过若干年的建设，一座清洁、安宁、满城尽绿的现代宜居城市出现在这片古老的土地上。

扬州名胜古迹和古街名宅众多。政府十分注重老城区的历史建筑和历史街区的保护、改造与利用，并取得很大的经济效益和社会效益。在保护老城区的过程中，扬州市政府认真继承和弘扬扬州传统人居文化，彰显传统民居建筑特色，并翻建老街巷，整治和改善居住环境。如今，老城区的市民延续着传统的居住和生活方式，生活得更加舒适，老城区的人文气息也更加浓厚。

这几年，扬州还实施了文化名城解读工程和文化博览城建设工程。这些文化景观，既讲述着城市的历史，展示着城市的文化，又充满生机地延续着城市的文明。众多博物馆的建成，无疑使扬州成为一座更宜修身养性的城市。

· 古城传统民居

新城生态新楼居

近年来，扬州城市基础设施建设取得了飞跃发展，绝大部分道路进行了拓宽改造、延伸，并新建了许多大道，城市交通状况明显改观。体育公园、会展中心和学校、医院等一系列公用设施和服务设施的兴建与改造，为市民提供了更加优质的公共服务，让市民更好地享受到了城市经济文化发展的成果。

· 扬州文昌路

扬州已成为广大市民共同的美好家园。在新城区，扬州的商品房建设特别强调以人为本，住宅建筑密度合理，以多层住宅为主，小高层和高层住宅为辅，确保绿化覆盖率，努力呈现当代扬州的居住特色。扬州还建立了

An Ancient City with an Artistic Atmosphere and Ancient Dwellings

After reform and opening-up, in the new historical period, Yangzhou defines itself as a historical and cultural city, a major tourist destination with rich traditions, as well as an eco-friendly garden city suitable for living. Now, after many years of construction, a modern city stands on this ancient land, clean, peaceful and green.

Yangzhou has numerous historic places of interest and beautiful scenic spots as well as many ancient streets and houses. The government pays great attention to and has made significant progress in the protection, transformation and utilization of historical buildings and areas. In the process of protecting this ancient city, they have not only been inheriting and preserving the traditional residential culture of Yangzhou and highlighting its unique architectural features, but also rebuilding the old streets, as well as renovating and improving living conditions. Today, the old town residents are enjoying a more comfortable life while keeping their traditional style of living. The old town in the city now radiates an even stronger artistic atmosphere.

In the recent years, Yangzhou has also implemented a project for cultural interpretation and a project for building the Culture Expo City. These cultural sites tell people the city history, demonstrate the city culture, and promote the city civilization. The numerous museums in Yangzhou undoubtedly contribute to its image of a city appropriate for self-cultivation.

Ecological Newly-built Dwellings

In the recent years, Yangzhou has been making great progress in its infrastructure construction; a vast majority of roads were widened, extended and repaired, and many new roads were built. Thus, city traffic conditions have been greatly improved. The construction and renovation of a series of public facilities like the Sports Park, the Convention Center, schools, and hospitals makes it possible to provide better services for the citizens, allowing them to enjoy the results of the city's economic and cultural development.

Yangzhou makes a conscious effort to provide quality housing to the general public. In the new city area, commercial housing construction is human-oriented, emphasizing appropriate population density in residential areas. Apartment buildings are mostly multi-storied, while high-rises and skyscrapers are few, so as to ensure an adequate rate of green space and create modern residential areas. In order to improve the living conditions of the disadvantaged groups and migrant workers, Yangzhou has also set

由经济适用房、定销房和限价商品房组成的住房保障体系，为城市弱势群体、外来人员群体等改善了居住条件，使他们享有适当住房，为他们更好地生活打下了良好的基础。

扬州完整的古城风貌和优良的人居环境吸引了越来越多的人来前来旅游、居住。近几年，扬州接待境内外游客人次和城市旅游总收入每年保持20%左右的增幅；来扬州定居的外地人口逐年增加，每年的新建商品房中有近四分之一为外地人所购买。

水城处处树和花

香径绿叶红花，小桥流水人家。漫步扬州，你随处可见蔚蓝如洗的天空、碧水潺潺的河流、绿意盎然的园林和鸟语花香的住宅小区。

扬州自古是一座水城。近十几年来，扬州加强水环境整治和水景观建设，使古城重现“水城共生”景象。水中树影婆娑、桥影荡漾，水中有飞鸟身影掠过。人们可以亲水、戏水，以水为友，以水为邻，感受水的魅力。

近年来扬州市区每年新增绿地100万平方米以上，建设了100多处城市绿地公园，城市绿化覆盖率达47.72%，人均公园绿地面积超过13平方米，居民处处可推窗见绿，形成了“城在园中、园在城中”的城市特色。

银杏、柳树是扬州的市树，琼花、芍药是扬州的市花，《茉莉花》是扬州的市歌。扬州自古就是出产名花的地方，“十里栽花算种田”，郊区的农民有许多家种花卖花。在城里，街边、楼边、河边、院子里、围墙上、窗台上和露台上、甚至楼顶，到处长满了花草。花是善和美的象征，一生一世生活于鲜花的天地中，人的身体会更健康，生命会更长寿，心地会更善良，性格会更完美。

· 银杏

· 柳树

up a housing guarantee system, which consists of economically affordable houses, a rationed housing market and commercial houses with fixed prices, making sure that they have adequate housing, which helps lay a good foundation for their better life.

The ancient style and good living conditions of Yangzhou have attracted more and more tourists and residences. In the recent years, Yangzhou has received tourists both from home and abroad at the rising rate of 20% annually. The number of people who come to settle down in Yangzhou has been increasing year by year. Annually, about a quarter of the new commercial housing are purchased by new comers.

A City on the Water with Trees and Flowers Everywhere

There are sweet-smelling pathways lined with greenery and red flowers on both sides, with houses and small bridges under which runs clear creak water. Taking a walk in Yangzhou, you may have a view of green gardens under a blue sky with gurgling streams and residential districts with birds singing and flowers emanating sweet fragrance.

Since ancient times, Yangzhou has been a city on the water. In the recent years, Yangzhou has been focusing more on regulating the water environment and creating a water landscape, making sure that this ancient city embodies the concept of "water—city co-existence", in which shadowy trees dance, reflections of bridges ripple and birds' shadows flit past quickly in the water. People live in harmony with water: play in water, make friends with water, learn from water and feel the charm of water.

In the recent years, the public green space in urban Yangzhou has grown by over 1,000,000 square meters annually, and more than 100 city parks have been constructed. The green coverage rate has reached 42.5% and the average green land area 13 square meters per person. When the residents open their windows, greenery will come into sight; hence, the distinguishing city characteristic of "city in the park, park in the city".

Ginkgo and willow are the city trees of Yangzhou, Qionghua flower and peony are its city flowers, and *Jasmine Flower* is the city song. Yangzhou has been growing famous flowers since ancient times. As a poem goes, "Ten-mile flower growing equals grain farming". At present, in the outskirts of Yangzhou quite a lot of flower farmers make a living by growing flowers. In the city, people grow flowers on both sides of the street, next to buildings, on river banks, inside courtyards, on top of walls, on windowsills and balconies, and even on top of buildings. Flowers symbolize kindness and beauty. Living in the flowery world, people are sure to have a healthier life, enjoy longevity, become more virtuous and possess kind characters.

第二章
园林揽胜

扬州美景以园林胜，现今被保留下来的古典名园是其悠久历史文化最鲜活的代表。

扬州园林历史悠久，早在西汉，吴王刘濞就在广陵兴建园林了。到了唐代，扬州经济发达，出现了“园林多是宅，车马少于船”的盛况。清代是扬州园林修筑的另一高峰，曾有“扬州园林秀甲天下”的说法。清末，由于城市的衰落及战争的影响，扬州园林受到极大破坏。

新中国成立后，扬州园林得到了较好的保护与开发。瘦西湖、个园、何园、汪氏小苑、平山堂西园、文峰公园、小盘谷、冶春园等名园得到有效保护，获得了盎然生机；同时，盆景园、茱萸湾公园、竹西公园、二十四桥景区等园林也重现了昔日的繁盛景象。1996年，扬州成为首批“江苏省园林城市”，2003年获得了“国家园林城市”的称号。

扬州园林的总体风格是自然、含蓄、清新、雅健，常依天然形态，招山入园，借水成景，利用高超的叠石技艺，与厅、台、楼、榭、阁、舫、游廊、复道回廊等古典建筑进行巧妙组合，缀以名花、古木，形成了兼有北方之雄和南方之秀的特点。

Chapter II

Charms of Classical Yangzhou Gardens

Throughout history, Yangzhou has been famous for its gardens. Nowadays, the preserved classical gardens are the vivid representatives of the long history of Yangzhou.

Yangzhou gardens have a long history. As early as in the Western Han Dynasty, Liu Bi, King of the State of Wu, began to build gardens in Guangling. By the Tang Dynasty, Yangzhou enjoyed economic prosperity, with its splendor truly reflected in poems like "Vehicles and horses are fewer than the ships; most of the gardens are residences." In the Qing Dynasty came another high point of garden construction, which was reflected in a popular saying "Yangzhou gardens are the best in China." However, during the late Qing Dynasty, Yangzhou gardens were badly destroyed because of the city's decline and the wars.

Since the foundation of the People's Republic of China, Yangzhou gardens have been better protected and developed. Famous gardens like the Slender West Lake, Ge Garden, He Garden, Wang's Residence, Pingshan Hall West Park, Wengfeng Park, Small Valley and Yechun Garden are thriving under effective protection. Meanwhile, the Bonsai Garden, Mastixia Bay Park, Bamboo West Park, Twenty-four Bridge Scenic Spot have regained splendor. In 1996, Yangzhou became one of the first Garden Cities in Jiangsu Province and in 2003 it won the title of the National-level Garden City.

Yangzhou gardens are generally characterized as being natural, reserved, fresh and elegant. The design is usually based upon the principles of following the natural landscape, using rocks in the construction of gardens, incorporating pools, lakes, or rivers in a garden scene, combining the art of rock formations with halls, terraces, towers, waterside pavilions, multilayered pavilions, marble boats, verandas and double-layered galleries, and decorating gardens with famous flowers and ancient trees. In this way, the style of Yangzhou gardens can be characterized by combining the grandeur of North China and the delicacy of South China.

第一节　瘦西湖

瘦西湖风景区位于扬州市区西北，南大门位于大虹桥路，现有游览区面积123.6公顷左右。1988年瘦西湖被国务院列为国家重点风景名胜区，2010年被授予国家AAAAA级旅游景区。

· 瘦西湖

瘦西湖清瘦狭长，原名保障湖，水面长约4千米，宽不及100米，后因清代汪沆的诗句“垂杨不断接残芜，雁齿虹桥俨画图。也是销金一锅子，故应唤作瘦西湖”而名扬天下。隋唐时期，瘦西湖沿岸便陆续建园，历年各代经营沟通，因地制宜建造了很多建筑。特别是清代，众多富有的盐商纷纷在沿河两岸，不惜重金聘请造园名家，设计、构筑水上园林，形成了“两岸花柳全依水，一路楼台直到山”的美景。清代康熙、乾隆两代帝王六度南巡，均游览了瘦西湖。

瘦西湖风景区是我国湖上园林的杰出代表，其湖面曲折迤逦，虹桥、长堤春柳、徐园、四桥烟雨、白塔、小金山、钓鱼台、五亭桥、凫庄、二十四桥等景点，或依山傍水，或空架湖面，错落有致地掩映于清丽的水道之间。瘦西湖不仅有秀丽的自然风光，还蕴含着丰富的历史文化。

Section One The Slender West Lake

The Slender West Lake Scenic Spot lies in the northwestern part of Yangzhou, with its south gate facing Great Rainbow Bridge Road. It covers an area of about 123.6 hectares. The Slender West Lake was named a National Key Scenic Spot in 1988 and National AAAAA Tourist Area in 2010.

The Slender West Lake used to be a long river named the Baozhang Lake, which is 4 kilometers in length and less than 100 meters in width. A famous poet Wang Hang in the Qing Dynasty once composed a poem, from which the Slender West Lake gets its present name and to which it owes its great fame both at home and abroad. The poem goes like this: "Drooping willows continuously connect with remnant thicket grass; with steps echeloning like flying cranes, the Great Rainbow Bridge is just like a landscape painting; the lake scenery is as beautiful as that of the West Lake; therefore it can be called 'the Slender West Lake'." During the Sui and Tang Dynasties, many gardens were built along the Slender West Lake. Following the lines of the natural landscape, a large number of buildings along the moats were constructed in different locations during different periods. Especially during the Qing Dynasty, many rich salt merchants spared no expense in recruiting outstanding garden designers and opting for large-scale construction of the landscape garden upon the lake. Since then, a splendid view of "willows and flowers on the embankments wave all along the waterside, while the road with pavilions and terraces leads up to the hillside" has been created. Emperors Kangxi and Qianlong of the Qing Dynasty both visited the Slender West Lake during their respective six inspection tours to the south of the Yangtze River.

The Slender West Lake Scenic Spot is an outstanding representative of the lake gardens in China. The narrow and meandering waterways connect many scenic spots, including the Great Rainbow Bridge, Spring Willows along the Long Bank, Xuyuan Garden, Four Bridges in Mist & Rain, the White Pagoda, the Small Golden Hill, the Fishing Terrace, the Five-pavilion Bridge, Fu Manor and the Twenty-four Bridge. They are scattered in picturesque disorder, some built on the slope along the water, others rising over the water, with their silhouettes reflected in the lake. In a word, the Slender West Lake not only represents the beauty of natural landscape, but also embodies the richness of its history and culture.

大虹桥

“扬州好，第一是虹桥”，《梦香词》这首词描述的就是扬州的大虹桥。大虹桥周围景色迷人，曾吸引了众多文人雅士在此切磋诗文，留下了许多珍贵的墨迹和动人的故事。

现在的大虹桥是一座三孔拱形石桥，桥身曲线优美，姿态端庄，横卧于瘦西湖碧波之上，远望犹如蓝天上的一道彩虹。如果把瘦西湖比作一位古典美人，是大虹桥揭开了她的盖头；如果把瘦西湖比作一部长剧，是大虹桥拉开了她的帷幕。走过大虹桥，瘦西湖的南大门便在眼前了。

· 大虹桥

长堤春柳

· 长堤春柳

一跨入瘦西湖的南大门，就见到一条似乎没有尽头的长堤，左侧是芳草萋萋的山坡，右侧是波光粼粼的湖水，三步一桃，五步一柳。一年中，长堤的春天最美，在融融的春风中，桃花缤纷艳丽，柳丝婀娜起舞，长堤犹如挂满彩色珠帘的画廊。三月烟雨天的长堤更美，柳丝新绿，桃木含苞，点点春光都笼罩在氤氲的烟雨中，远处的亭台楼阁如海市蜃楼，漫步于长堤，如梦如幻，好像是在轻烟似的薄纱中穿行。有人说，这就是“烟花三月”的意境。

The Great Rainbow Bridge

The Great Rainbow Bridge stands for Yangzhou's fairness, as is eulogized in the poem of *Dreaming Fragrance*, to the effect that "The scene of the Rainbow Bridge is the most enchanting in the beautiful Yangzhou", and it was the venue for parties held by literary men, who usually composed and exchanged their poems and articles, leaving us many precious literary masterpieces and touching stories.

The present-day Great Rainbow Bridge is a three-arch stone bridge with beautiful curving lines. It stands over the green waves of the Slender West Lake, looking from a distance like a rainbow hanging high in the sky. If the Slender West Lake is compared to a classic beauty, it is the Great Rainbow Bridge who pulls up her veil; if compared to a long drama, it is the Great Rainbow Bridge who opens its curtain. After crossing the Great Rainbow Bridge, the tourists will find themselves in front of the south gate of the Slender West Lake.

Spring Willows along the Long Bank

As soon as you enter the south gate of the Slender West Lake, you will see a long bank seemingly stretching into infinity, with the green hillsides on the left and sparkling lake on the right. The long bank is lined with peach trees and willow trees, which creates breath-taking beauty in spring. With colorful peach trees in full bloom and willow branches dancing in the spring breeze, the long bank looks like a gallery decorated with colorful pearl shades. Particularly on misty and rainy days in March, when peach trees are in bud and willow trees are newly green, all the beautiful scenery is shrouded under the mist of rain. The distant gazebos, terraces, towers, and multilayered pavilions are like a mirage. In the gauze-like mist tourists wander along the bank, enjoying the charm of early spring. Here lies the irresistible charm of "the mist and flowers in spring".

徐园

长堤的尽头便是徐园，它是辛亥革命时期军阀徐宝山的祠堂。徐园中有一馆、一榭、一亭，外有曲水，内有池塘，花木竹石，恰到好处。园中“听鹂馆”取名来自唐朝诗人杜甫的“两只黄鹂鸣翠柳，一行白鹭上青天”的诗意。听鹂馆门前的两口大铁镬（镬读hùo），是1500多年前的镇水神器，说明了当时扬州冶炼业的发达程度。

· 徐园

关于徐园，至今流传着一个徐老虎和风先生的故事。徐宝山生性残忍，又属虎，江湖上畏之如虎，故有绰号“徐老虎”。风先生原名吉亮工，是清末民初扬州著名的书法家，自称为“莽书生”、“风先生”。徐老虎不通文墨，请风先生为他提写“徐园”二字，字是写了，但“园”字行笔精妙，人们都说这个字的形状像一只笼中的老虎。

小金山

穿过徐园，跨过小虹桥，便来到了小金山。小金山原名“长春岭”，乾隆年间在湖中堆砌而成。扬州文人雅士将长春岭与镇江金山相比，觉得前者虽小但风景秀美，不逊于金山，因此称之为“小金山”。小金山是瘦西湖中最大的岛屿，也是湖上建筑最密集的地方，分布有风亭、吹台、琴室、木樨书屋、棋室、月观等景观。其中，风亭位于小金山之巅，吸天地之精华，吐山川之灵气，亭中有对联为证：“风月无边，到此胸怀何似；亭台依旧，羡他烟水全收。”

· 小金山

Xuyuan Garden

At the end of the bank stands Xuyuan Garden, which was initially a memorial temple of a warlord named Xu Baoshan during the Revolution of 1911. Xuyuan Garden is surrounded by the waters of the lake, with a hall, a waterside pavilion, a gazebo, and a pool inside. It has carefully planned layout of flowers, trees, bamboos and rockeries. An important building inside the garden is the Hall of Listening to Orioles, so named after a famous poem composed by Du Fu, a great poet of the Tang Dynasty. "A couple of orioles are warbling in the verdant willows. Meanwhile a line of egrets into the blue sky do soar." In front of the hall, there are two big iron caldrons. According to the legend, the caldrons were used to suppress the dragons that caused floods as early as 1,500 years ago; they are the relics representing the advanced level of metallurgy of Yangzhou at that time.

There is a story about Xu Baoshan and Mr Feng when mentioning Xuyuan Garden. Xu Baoshan was very cruel and built his career on killing. He was born in the Tiger year of the lunar calendar, so people who were terrified of him gave him a nickname "Tiger Xu". Mr Feng, also known as Ji Lianggong, was an outstanding Yangzhou calligrapher in the Qing Dynasty. He called himself Mr Mang or Mr Feng. It was said that Tiger Xu was not well-educated, so he asked Mr Feng to write two Chinese characters "Xu Yuan" for his garden. The character "Yuan" was written exquisitely and smartly. People say that the shape of the character "园" is very much like a tiger in the cage.

The Small Golden Hill

Across Xuyuan Garden stands a bridge called the Small Rainbow Bridge leading to the Small Golden Hill. It used to be named Eternal Spring Ridge, and was built in the lake during the reign of Qianlong in the Qing Dynasty. Comparing Eternal Spring Ridge with the Golden Hill in Zhenjiang, the literati in Yangzhou felt that although it was small, its scenery was as beautiful as that of the Golden Hill. Therefore, they named it the Small Golden Hill. The Small Golden Hill is the largest islet in the Slender West Lake, and also the place housing most of the buildings in the scenic area. Among them, the Wind Pavilion, the Blowing Terrace, the Harp Chamber, the Osmanthus Fragrance Study House, the Chess Room and the Moon-viewing Pavilion are located here. Among them, the Wind Pavilion is situated at the top of the hill, uniting the essence of the Heaven and the Earth, as manifested by one of the couplets inscribed inside, "The wonders of the moonlight and wind are boundless; here I am getting as broad-minded as the immense scenery. The pavilion remains the same over centuries; how I envy its command of the superb panorama of the surrounding mist and waters."

钓鱼台

· 钓鱼台

钓鱼台又名“吹台”，原来是演奏丝竹乐器的地方。相传乾隆皇帝曾在此钓鱼，陪同的盐商悄悄选了几个水性好的水手带着活龙鱼潜到水下。水手们举着荷叶，靠荷茎来换气，乾隆的鱼杆一落，他们就将活龙鱼挂上钩，使得乾隆龙心大悦。

钓鱼台位于湖心长堤的顶端，是一个黄墙翘角的方亭。钓鱼台三面临湖，南、北、西各有一个月洞，在西边的圆洞中可看到五亭桥横卧在波光粼粼的湖面上，在南边的椭圆形洞中看到白塔耸立云端，在北边的月洞中则见到绿树掩映的桂花厅。这种奇妙的“框景”手法是中国名亭建筑的一绝，赢得了“三星拱照”的佳称。

五亭桥

如果把瘦西湖比做一位婀娜多姿的少女，那么五亭桥就是少女身上那条华美的腰带。五亭桥不仅是瘦西湖的标志，也是扬州城的象征。五亭桥建于清乾隆年间，至今已有200多年的历史。

五亭桥又名“莲花桥”，是一座别致的拱形石桥，长50多米，横跨湖面。桥上建有五座挺拔秀丽的风亭，亭上有宝顶，亭内绘有天花，亭外挂有风铃，就像五朵冉冉出水的并蒂莲花。五亭桥的桥下有大小不一的15个桥洞，洞洞相连，洞洞相通。空灵的拱顶桥洞配上敦实的桥基，桥基的直线配上桥洞的曲线，比例自然流畅，效果和谐统一，是古今中外桥梁建筑史上的杰作。现代著名桥梁专家茅以升曾这样评价：“中国最古老的桥是赵州桥，最壮美的桥是卢沟桥，最具艺术美的桥就是扬州的五亭桥。”

· 五亭桥

The Fishing Terrace

The Fishing Terrace is also called the Blowing Terrace, where traditional stringed and woodwind instruments used to be played. Legend has it that Emperor Qianlong once fished here. To satisfy him, the accompanying salt merchants of Yangzhou secretly selected several good divers and sent them carrying live fish down into the water. The divers were covered with lotus leaves, breathing through lotus stalks. Whenever the emperor cast his line, the divers would put the live fish onto his hook. In this way, Qianlong couldn't be more pleased as the live fish took the bait immediately as he dropped the fishing rod.

The Fishing Terrace lies at the end of the long bank stretching to the center of the lake. It is a square pavilion with yellow walls and upturned roof corners. The terrace is surrounded by water on three sides, namely in the south, north and west, each side with a moon gate. From the west moon gate, one can see the Five-pavilion Bridge over the sparkling lake; from the south moon gate the towering White Pagoda; from the north moon gate the Guihua (Osmanthus) Hall nestling in the shade of green trees. This unique technique is called "borrowed scene" in Chinese gardening. Thus, this pavilion was aptly named "Three Stars Shining".

The Five-pavilion Bridge

If the Slender West Lake is compared to a graceful young lady, the Five-pavilion Bridge is like a beautiful belt worn on her waist. The Five-pavilion Bridge is not only the symbol of the Slender West Lake, but that of Yangzhou as well. Built during Qianlong's reign in the Qing Dynasty, it has a history of over 200 years.

The Five-pavilion Bridge, also named the Lotus Bridge, is an elegant stone arch bridge, which runs for more than 50 meters across the lake. Built on the bridge are five wind pavilions, each wearing a crown on the top. There are ceiling decorations inside the pavilions and wind-bells hanging outside. They look like five lotus flowers rising slowly out of water. The lower part contains 15 bridge openings of different sizes, which are interconnected. The airy arched openings juxtapose the sturdy foundations, while the straight lines complement the curvy lines in a smooth and natural proportion, achieving a balanced and harmonious visual effect. It is a masterpiece in the history of bridge architecture both at home and abroad. The famous Chinese bridge engineering expert Mao Yisheng once commented, "The most ancient bridge in China is Zhaozhou Bridge; the most splendid, Lugou Bridge; the most elegant and artistic, the Five-pavilion Bridge in Yangzhou."

白塔

相传1784年，乾隆皇帝第六次坐船游览扬州瘦西湖时，从水上看到五亭桥一带的景色，不由遗憾地说："只可惜少了一座白塔，不然这儿看起来和北海的琼岛春阴就像极了。"说者无心，听者有意，财大气粗的扬州盐商当即花了十万两银子跟太监买来北海白塔的图样，当晚连夜建成了一座白塔。这就是在扬州流传至今的"一夜造塔"的故事。

· 白塔

白塔高27.5米，下面是束腰须弥塔座，八面四角，每面三龛，龛内雕刻着十二生肖像。和北海白塔的厚重稳健不同，扬州白塔比例匀称，亭亭玉立，与身边的五亭桥相映成趣。

二十四桥

现在的二十四桥景区为1990年根据史料复建而成。"二十四桥"出自唐代著名诗人杜牧的诗句，"青山隐隐水迢迢，秋尽江南草未凋；二十四桥明月夜，玉人何处教吹萧。"

二十四桥景区由熙春台、玲珑界、小李将军画本、望春楼、落帆栈道、单孔拱桥、九曲桥及吹箫亭等组合而成。主景单孔拱桥长24米，宽2.4米，有栏柱24根，台级24层，处处都与二十四桥相呼应，桥上围着汉白玉栏杆，洁白的桥栏板上刻有"彩云追月"的浮雕，桥墩临水处有植满鲜花的花台。

月明之夜，亲历其境，那如梦似幻的感觉更增添了"天下三分明月夜，二分无赖是扬州"的神秘和意趣。

The White Pagoda

Legend has it that during his sixth inspection tour of Yangzhou in 1784, Emperor Qianlong was traveling by boat and enjoying the scenery of the Five-pavilion Bridge when he said to the accompanying salt merchants, "The landscape of the Lotus Bridge looks much like that of Beihai Park, but lacks a white pagoda." His casual remark was picked up by the wealthy salt merchants of Yangzhou. In order to delight the emperor, they spent one hundred thousand taels of silver buying a sketch of the Beihai White Pagoda from a eunuch and put up a fake white pagoda overnight. The story of making a white pagoda overnight has been passed down from generation to generation in Yangzhou.

The White Pagoda stands 27.5 meters tall; there is a slim-waist Xumi Base (the landmark of Chinese ancient architectural base) under the pagoda. It is an octahedral quadrangle with three shrines on each side. Contained in them are 12 symbolic animals of each lunar year. Unlike the massive White Pagoda in Beijing, the White Pagoda in Yangzhou is slim and graceful, casting beautiful reflection along with the Five-pavilion Bridge.

The Twenty-four Bridge

The present complex of the Twenty-four Bridge Scenic Spot was restored in 1990 based on the recorded sketches of the Twenty-four Bridge. The ancient Twenty-four Bridge became famous because of a poem composed by Du Mu of the Tang Dynasty. It goes like this: "Dim the mountains, far away the waters, autumn is approaching its end in the South, with withered grass in view. The moon has lit up the Twenty-four Bridge in the town. Where is the sweet girl who played the flute for you?"

The Twenty-four Bridge Scenic Spot consists of the Xichun Terrace, the Delicate Flower Field, the Sketchbook of General Li Jr, the Spring Viewing Building, the Sail-lowering Boardwalk, the Arch Bridge, the Zigzag Bridge (the Nine-Bend Bridge) and the Flute-playing Pavilion. The Arch Bridge is the main building of the complex. It is 24 meters long and 2.4 meters wide, with 24 steps and 24 parapets of white jade, giving the complex its name. The cross-sections of the white-jade guard rails are engraved with a relief sculpture "Colorful Clouds Chasing the Moon". Right next to the water, four flower stands with flowers in full bloom are symmetrically placed on the pier of the bridge. Taking a walk under the full moon, one personally experiences the ephemeral beauty of the landscape that inspired the Tang-dynasty poem: "There are three parts of moonlight in the world, and two parts of them are in Yangzhou."

熙春台是二十四桥景区的主体建筑，它选用了绿色的琉璃瓦，与五亭桥黄瓦红梁、白塔的玉体金顶形成了强烈的视觉对比。“熙春”一词出自老子《道德经》中的“众人熙熙，如登春台”，意指熙春台前人来人往、摩肩接踵的热闹场面。相传当年扬州盐商曾在这里为乾隆皇帝祝寿，所以这一景又被称为“春台祝寿”。

· 二十四桥

万花园

万花园是瘦西湖的子景区，是根据《扬州府志》记载的宋代“万花园”复建，总投资约1.8亿元，于2007年4月18日向游人开放。

· 万花园

万花园西、南两面与瘦西湖相邻，北临小运河，东靠平山堂路，总面积约44.2公顷。万花园强调与瘦西湖沿线景点的融合、衔接和过渡，强调“万花”主题，具有花事、博览、观奇、体验、智趣、休闲、教育、生态、娱乐、审美十大功能。万花园四季有花，最佳赏园时间为4月中旬至5月初。

万花园依托瘦西湖的历史文化背景，以花文化为主题，以古典历史名园为线索，先后恢复和新建了“石壁流淙”、“锦泉花屿”、“醉月飞琼”等景点。其中“石壁流淙”是万花园内的点睛之作，景点由“水竹居”、“阆风堂”等三组建筑和一组黄石假山组成。

The main structure of the Twenty-four Bridge Scenic Spot is the Xichun Terrace, whose green glaze roof tiles create a striking visual contrast with the yellow tiles and red beams of the Five-pavilion Bridge, as well as the white jade and red crown of the White Pagoda. "Xichun" originates from the line in *Tao Te Ching* by Lao Tzu, an ancient Chinese philosopher, "All men are joyous and beaming, as though climbing the Spring Terrace." It also refers to the crowds in front of the Xichun Terrace. According to the legend, the salt merchants of Yangzhou held a grand ceremony here to celebrate the birthday of Emperor Qianlong, giving it another name Birthday Celebration on the Terrace.

The Multicolored Garden

The present-day Multicolored Garden, as a part of the Slender West Lake Scenic Spot, is a reconstruction of the Song-dynasty Multicolored Garden according to *The Records of Yangzhou Prefecture*. The total investment reaches about 180 million yuan. It has been open to the public since April, 18th, 2007.

The Multicolored Garden faces the Slender West Lake in the west and the south, and borders the Small Canal in the north, and the Pingshan Hall Road in the east. It covers an area of about 44.2 hectares. The Multicolored Garden is best enjoyed in combination with the other scenic spots along the Slender West Lake. It highlights the theme of "flowers of every kind" and serves the top ten functions of blooming seasons, wonder-watching, experience, knowledge, leisure, education, ecology, entertainment, and aesthetics. In this garden, different kinds of flowers bloom throughout the year. The best time to visit the garden is from the mid-April to the beginning of May.

The Multicolored Garden is based on the historical and cultural background of the Slender West Lake. It emphasizes horticulture—drawing inspiration from classical and historical gardens. More scenic spots like the Water Splashes along the Stone Wall, the Jin Quan Flower Islet, the Drunken Moon Flying over Qiong Gate have been restored or newly built. The most outstanding among them is the Water Splashes along the Stone Wall, consisting of a complex of the Fishscale Bamboo Residence, the Lang Feng Hall, and a group of Huang stone rockeries.

第二节　个园

个园位于扬州古城的东北隅，是江南私家园林的杰出代表，被誉为中国四大名园之一，是全国重点文物保护单位、国家AAAA级旅游景区。清代嘉庆年间，两淮盐商商总黄至筠在明代寿芝园的旧址上扩建而成住宅园林，因主人爱竹，根据清代袁枚"月映竹成千个字"诗句中的寓意，将园子命名为"个园"。个园园记中记载，园主认为竹子象征着君子之风——"本固"、"心虚"、"体直"、"节贞"，意思是说做人要讲根本，树立德行；处世要讲虚心，谦虚谨慎；为人要讲正直和气节。

· 个园

个园景区大致可分为中部花园区、南部住宅区、北部品种竹观赏区三个部分，占地约2.3公顷。个园以假山堆叠精巧而著名，它以笋石、湖石、黄石、宣石筑成春夏秋冬四季假山，其叠石艺术高超，与翠竹、奇花、异木、亭阁相得益彰，令人叹为观止，被园林泰斗陈从周先生誉为"国内孤例"。

四季假山

个园的中部花园以假山堆叠精巧而名扬天下，它利用不同颜色、不同类型的天然石材，按顺时针方向堆砌成春、夏、秋、冬四季山景，表达出了"春景艳冶而如笑，夏山苍翠而如滴，秋山明净而如妆，冬景惨淡而如睡"和"春山宜游，夏山宜看，秋山宜登，冬山宜居"的意境。

Section Two Ge Garden

As an outstanding representative of private gardens in Jiangnan (South-of-Yangtze-River region), one of the top four famous gardens in China, an important national-level cultural heritage and a National AAAA Tourist Area, Ge Garden is situated in the northeast of the ancient Yangzhou city. It was built on the basis of the Shouzhi Garden of the Ming Dynasty by Huang Zhijun, head of Salt Ministry in the Huai River Area during the reign of Emperor Jiaqing in the Qing Dynasty. Huang loved bamboo, and according to the poet Yuan Mei in the Qing Dynasty, "The shape of bamboo leaves resemble that of Chinese character "ge" (个) in the moonlight", thus the garden got its name. According to the gardening records of Ge Garden, the owner of the garden associated the noble quality of bamboo with men possessing perfect virtues and noble character. Bamboo is known for its firm roots, inside hollowness, upright position and joints in its appearance, which implies a noble person should possess the virtues of firm and indomitable spirit, humility, unselfishness and upright integrity.

The Ge Garden Scenic Spot, covering about 2.3 hectares, is mainly divided into three sections: the garden in the central part, the residence in the southern part, and the bamboo viewing zone in the northern part. The garden is well-known for its exquisitely piled stones, especially its seasonal rockeries—Bamboo stone for spring, Taihu stone for summer, Huang stone for autumn and Xuan stone for winter. The rockeries in the garden are designed by resorting to stone-piling, harmoniously integrating the artificial hills with green bamboos, rare flowers, exotic trees and serene pavilions, which never fails to make a lasting impression on visitors. Therefore, the rockeries were appraised as "the only case in the country" by Mr Chen Congzhou—the national authority on garden architecture.

Four Seasons Rockeries

The center of the garden is famous for the exquisitely placed rockeries. Rocks of different hues and shapes are used to represent scenes of the four seasons in a clockwise circle of the Spring Hill, the Summer Hill, the Autumn Hill and the Winter Hill. Each of the rockeries shows a different poetic and artistic aspect of the four seasons. It can be described as "The rockery in spring is flamboyant like a bright smile, in summer is

春山在花园的南部，与住宅相通。住宅北侧是一段砌有花窗的白墙，墙上正中开一个月洞门，门上石额刻着“个园”。园门两侧各有一个方形花坛，花坛内种满翠竹，竹丛中插入七八支用白果岩寓意的绿色石笋，犹如雨后春笋破土而出，点出了初春的意境。过“个园”洞门，便见到“十二生肖闹春图”。它用形态别致的太湖石，沿花墙由东向西，堆成各种生肖动物形态，如微微昂首的长蛇、负重向前的耕牛、活泼可爱的小狗、聪明调皮的猴子、长啸山林的猛虎、乖巧温顺的玉兔等，好似众多动物的大聚会，展示了春回大地、万物复苏的热闹景象。

· 春意盎然

· 苍翠欲滴

· 鱼骨石

夏山在园子西北角的荷花池畔，一座苍翠玲珑的太湖石假山掩映在数棵高大的广玉兰和枫杨之中。夏山精心选择了具备瘦、透、漏、皱特点的青灰色太湖石堆砌而成，表达了江南山水的婉约柔美。夏山脚下的池塘中睡莲点点，展现了夏日中生命的苍翠与活力。水上架着一座曲桥，曲桥前面侧立一湖石，自下而上有三个近圆形的孔洞，如剔净的鱼骨，所以被称为“鱼骨石”，这就是个园的“镇园之宝”。从池塘东侧走过曲桥，可进入夏山石屋。夏山顶建有四角小亭，名“鹤亭”，相传这里是主人养鹤的地方。亭前有一株古柏，枝条虬曲，增添了夏山的葱郁气氛。

verdant like sparkling dewdrops, in autumn is clean like light makeup, and in winter, it is pale like a sleeping beauty." Also "the Spring Hill is for visit, the Summer Hill is for sight, the Autumn Hill is for climbing, and the Winter Hill is for residence."

The Spring Hill is located in the south part of the garden and is connected to the residence, to the north of which stands a white wall with rosettes. In the midst of the wall is a moon-shaped gate above which two Chinese characters "个园" are engraved. At the gate of the garden, there are square parterres on both sides with slender bamboos and several unevenly distributed stone bamboos in them. The stone bamboo shoots in the grove create an impression of spring vitality. Going through the gate, one will encounter twelve blocks of Taihu stone, shaped like the twelve animals of Chinese Zodiac. You may see a snake with its head held high, a hard-working ox pulling a plough, a lovely playful puppy, a smart naughty monkey, a fierce tiger in the wild, or a cute timid rabbit. Standing along the tracery wall from east to west, the twelve animals come together to celebrate the return of spring.

The Summer Hill is located near the lotus pool bank in the northwest of the garden. Here a verdant Taihu rockery is surrounded by several big magnolias and Chinese ash trees. In the Summer Hill, cinereous Taihu stones are used to impress the visitors with their "thinness and transparency, creases and holes", manifesting the elegance of South China landscape. Beneath the rockery, the pool is dotted with water lilies that become dark-green and vibrant in summer. There is a zigzag bridge above the water. In front of the bridge stands a block of Taihu stone with three holes from high to low. This Treasure of the Garden looks like fishbone, earning the name Fishbone Stone. Crossing the zigzag bridge from the east of the pool, one can enter the rock house in the Summer Hill. On top of the Summer Hill is the well-known Crane Pavilion, a square pavilion, where it is said that its owner used to raise cranes. In front of the pavilion stands an ancient lush cypress that adds to the verdant atmosphere of the Summer Hill.

由夏山向东，是一座气势不凡的长楼，这是园中最大的建筑——“抱山楼”。楼上、楼下各七个房间，沿楼廊向东走，可直达个园假山的精华——秋山。抱山楼在空间上连接夏山与秋山，长廊尤如手臂抱两山于胸前。游人漫步廊道，不知不觉就从夏走到了秋，所以此廊被戏称为“时空隧道”。

·层林尽染

秋山在园林东北角，用红褐色的黄石堆叠而成。秋山高峻陡峭，雄伟壮丽，是个园中最高的地方，登秋山俯瞰，满园景色尽收眼底。秋山峰顶有一个“拂云亭”，意思是人站在亭中，几乎可以拂到天上的云彩。秋山的山洞复杂，由上而下，由外而内，盘旋曲折，山洞中有石室，里面放有石桌、石床、石凳。秋山的山道险峻，两山陡岩之间有天桥、石梁相连，人走在山道上，移步换景，引人入胜。秋山的植物以枫树为多，每当夕阳西下，黄石丹枫，人行其间仿佛置身于秋日山林。秋山的最南部是丛书楼，山与楼巧妙结合，楼成了秋山最优雅的收尾。从山间石阶可直至楼上，它避开了园林中的主要路线，非常安静，是主人藏书、读书的地方。

·群狮嬉雪

冬山位于园内的南部，在高墙之下，用纯白的宣石堆叠而成，是园中占地面积最小的一组假山，但是构思却最为精巧独特、最富创意的一景。宣石的主要成份是石英，石质晶莹雪白，如残雪未消。冬石的形状似小狮子，远远看去，好像有许多小狮子在雪中嬉戏。山侧的几株腊梅更是烘托出了冬天的严寒。冬山前面的南墙开了24个“风音洞”，它代表了一年24个节气。风音洞所在的高墙与住宅的后墙之间是一条狭长的通道，风从高

Heading east of the Summer Hill, visitors may enjoy an extraordinarily long building, the main building of the garden: Bao Shanlou which means "a pavilion embracing the hills". The two-story pavilion houses seven rooms on each floor. Its wide long corridor will take people eastward right to the Autumn Hill—the essence of the Rockeries. Bao Shanlou functions as a bridge connecting the Summer Hill and the Autumn Hill. The corridor looks like the arms that are embracing the two hills. People step into "autumn" while walking leisurely down the corridor, thus the corridor is nicknamed "the time tunnel".

The Autumn Hill lies in the northeast of the garden and is made of piled reddish-brown Huang stones. As the highest spot in the garden, the Autumn Hill is remarkable for its towering cliffs and magnificent scenery. From the top of the hill people can enjoy to the fullest the grand sight of the whole garden. On its peak stands Fuyun Pavilion, which means that by standing on the platform of the pavilion, people can stand next to the clouds and almost touch them. The elaborate stone caves wind deep into the Autumn Hill. In either upper caves or lower ones, there are stone rooms. The stone rooms are decorated with stone desks, stone beds and stone benches. The paths along the way are arduous due to the fact that the towering cliffs are connected by bridges or stone beams. Moving along the paths, tourists will be refreshed by the ever changing scenes that never tire eyes. The Autumn Hill is covered with maple trees that change colors in late autumn. When the setting sun sheds its light on the Huang stones and red maple leaves, people will experience the splendor of forests in autumn. In the southern part of the Autumn Hill hides the Study Building. The hill and the building are ingeniously combined so that the latter provides an elegant finishing touch to the hill. By climbing the stone stairs which lead upward away from the main tour route, people will find themselves upstairs in the Study Building, where its owner used to read and store books.

The Winter Hill lies in the south of the garden. Round snow-white Xuan stones are piled up against the lofty walls. Though it occupies the least area of the four sets of rockeries, the Winter Hill scenery is of the greatest delicacy, creativity and originality. The main ingredient of Xuan stone is quartz, which is sparkling, crystal-clear and snow-white. When hills are covered with Xuan stone, the effect of accumulated snow and snow glimmering in the sunshine is guaranteed. The Winter Hill is remarkable for its shape. From the distance, the clustered stones look like many little lions playing in the snow field. Several winter sweet trees standing by the Winter Hill add to the winter chill. The most creative of the winter scenery is the south wall with 24 holes, which are called Whistling Holes. They stand for 24 Solar Terms in a year. A long narrow

墙窄巷中流过，速度会加快，穿过孔洞时呼呼作响，就像北风呼啸，加深了冬天的意境。最有趣的是冬山西墙上的两个“窥春洞”，把春景与冬景隔墙相连，透过孔洞可以看见春山，让人立刻产生“大地回春，周而复始”的联想，也让人想起英国著名抒情诗人雪莱的诗句：“冬天已经来临，春天还会远吗？”

豪门宅第

个园南部是主人的起居区，正门开在东关街上。传说个园鼎盛时期的住宅分别以“福、禄、寿、财、喜”为主题，五路豪宅纵向排列，原有房屋二百多间，虽然目前保存下来的只有三路，但一厅一堂、一梁一柱无不显示出园主生活的奢华与财力的雄厚。

东路建筑前后三进，檐口瓦头滴水及门窗阁扇，均用“鹿”的图案，寓意“禄”。东路建筑的第一进房屋为“清美堂”，是黄家接待一般性来客和处理日常事务的地方。“清美”意指以清为美，为官清正廉明，做人清清白白，是主人追求的境界。中间一进房屋为“楠木厅”，因大厅的梁柱为楠木而得名，此厅构造考究，规整宽敞，是宴请聚会的场所。最后一进房屋为厨房，现按传统厨房布局进行了恢复性陈设布置。民间传说黄至筠每天的早餐是燕窝、参汤、鸡蛋两只，其中一只鸡蛋就价值一两纹银。

· 楠木厅

中路建筑也分三进，前进为正厅，中进和后进为住宅，称之为“前厅后寝”。中路房屋的檐口瓦头滴水及门窗阁扇，均为倒挂蝙蝠，寓意“福到”。

passage connects the wall with 24 holes to the back wall of the residence. When the wind blows through the long narrow passage, it accelerates and whistles through the holes like roaring north wind, heightening the impression of winter. The most interesting aspect is that there are two holes in the west wall that separate the winter scenery from the spring one. The sight of the Spring Hill through the holes reminds the visitors of the Chinese saying "Spring returns to the earth year after year." and Shelley's lines "When winter comes, can spring be far behind?"

The Residential Area

In the southern part of Ge Garden lies Huang's residence, whose portal is in the Dongguan Street. The story goes that in the heyday of Ge Garden, five groups of houses with more than 200 rooms were ranged in tandem, according to their respective subject of the five Chinese fortunes—"fortune", "prosperity", "longevity", "wealth" and "happiness". Though today only three tandems of houses remain, either the hall or the main hall, either the beam or the pillar exhibits the owner's luxurious life and great wealth.

The eastern building complex is formed by three rows of houses, arranged around a quadrangle courtyard. All of its cornices, tiles, eaves doors, windows and wood panel gates are decorated with deer designs, representing "prosperity", for the Chinese characters "鹿" and "禄" (meaning "prosperity or government official's salary") are both pronounced *lu*. The house in the very front is named "Qingmei Hall". This hall used to be the place where the owner of the garden received his ordinary guests and dealt with routine. "Qingmei" literally means "appreciating incorruption", by which the owner made it clear to all that "being an honest and upright official and living a blameless life" was his motto and eternal pursuit. The house in the middle is called Nanmu Hall because its beams and pillars are made of Nanmu (Nanmu is a type of wood that was frequently used for boat building, architectural woodworking and wood art in China due to its resistance to humidity). This hall is elaborately designed and constructed, and is spacious and rectangular in shape. It used to be the place where the owner entertained his guests. The last house in the back row was used as a kitchen. Here visitors can see a restored traditional kitchen. As the legend goes, Huang Zhijun used to have bird's nest soup, ginseng soup, and two eggs for breakfast, and amazingly such an egg cost one tael silver ingot.

The middle building complex is also formed by three rows of houses. The front house once served as the main hall, the middle one and the back ones as living residences. That's the so-called "Front Hall Rear Chambers" in Chinese architecture of garden residence. Its cornices, tiles and eaves as

· 汉学堂

· 清颂堂

前进“汉学堂”是大宅门主厅，是黄家正式的接待场所。此厅屋梁为柏木架构，古朴雄浑，为明代建筑。汉学堂的中堂盈联为郑板桥所撰写的“咬定几句有用书可忘饮食，养成数杆新生竹直似儿孙”。中路中进是黄至筠次子黄奭（奭读shì）夫妇的居所。黄奭以勤奋博学而著名，留下了数百卷的著作。中路后进非常简朴，是黄至筠四子黄锡禧的居所。

西路住宅遗存主房也是前后三进，是黄家内眷生活的场所。西路房屋的檐口瓦头滴水是寿桃图案，门窗阁扇是仙鹤图案。前进房屋为“清颂堂”，此厅堂为杉木构架，是所有住宅中最高敞的厅堂，也是黄氏家族聚会、祭祀、排戏唱“堂会”的地方。中进与后进的房屋均为二层楼的住宅，称为“绣楼”。中间楼下西边最后一间是主人黄至筠的卧室，室内有藏宝洞，另一间是书房；楼下最东边房间有楼梯可直达二楼，楼上是内眷活动的场所，有绣房、儿童室等。西进楼下是正房卧室，楼上是闺房绣楼，有女儿的卧房、书房、娱乐室、沐浴房等。

well as its doors, windows and wood panel gates are decorated with the designs of bats flying upside down, meaning "happiness has arrived", for a bat (蝠) and "good fortune or happiness (福)" are visual puns and both pronounced *fu* in Chinese, also the Chinese character "倒" for "upside-down" and the Chinese character "到" meaning "to have arrived" are both pronounced *dao*. The main hall of the front house is Hanxue Hall, which served as the Huangs' formal reception place. This hall with its beams made of cypress is a Ming-dynasty building of grandeur and striking simplicity. Inside the parlour, there hangs an antithetical couplet written by the painter and calligrapher, Zheng Banqiao of the Qing Dynasty, which reads as follows: "Read good books with full concentration and grasp their essence; nurture the young bamboos into the ones with upright integrity and bring up the sons and grandsons likewise." The middle house used to be the residence of Huang Shi and his wife (Huang Shi was the second son of Huang Zhijun). Huang Shi was famous for his industry and profound learning, leaving us hundreds of volumes of works. The back house—built in a rather simple style—used to be the residence of Huang Xixi, the forth son of Huang Zhijun.

The western building complex is also formed by three rows of houses. This is where the female members of the Huang family lived. Its cornices, tiles and eaves are decorated with designs of peaches which symbolize longevity; its doors, windows and wood panel gates are decorated with the designs of cranes—also a symbol of longevity. Its front house, called Qingsong Hall, is a fir-framed hall, also the highest and the most spacious one in the building complexes. It used to be the venue where the family gathered to offer sacrifices to ancestors and rehearsed for their private theatrical shows or operas. The middle house and the back house are both two-story buildings, both named Embroidery Building. The western-most chamber downstairs in the back house used to be Huang Zhijun's bedroom, with a cave for treasures and a study. The eastern-most chamber has stairs that lead upstairs where there used to be the place for the wives and children of the Huang family, such as the embroidery rooms and children's rooms. The chamber downstairs in the back house used to be the bedroom of Huang Zhijun's first wife. The rooms upstairs were used as Huang Zhijun's daughters' boudoirs containing a bedroom, a study, a playroom, a bath room and so on.

竹园风情

竹是个园的精华和灵魂。1998年，个园在四季假山北侧建成品种竹观赏区，恢复了个园有竹“百种万竿”的历史原貌。现在，竹园占地面积1.2万平方米，有竹60多种，近20000竿。

从盐阜东路的北大门进入个园，迎面而来的就是万竿修竹，形同千军万马的绿色方阵，静时波澜不惊，动时风起潮涌，一派生气蓬勃的景象。千姿百态的竹林中还点缀着水池、亭阁，大致分为“土山竹林”、“品种观赏”、“映碧水榭”、“竹西佳处”四个区域。

竹的名称往往能反映其形色特征。龟甲竹是个园中最奇特的竹子，它的节片像龟甲又似龙鳞，凹凸有致，坚硬粗糙，与其他灵秀、俊逸的竹子相比，少了几分柔弱飘逸，多了几分刚强坚毅。

斑竹又名“湘妃竹”，绿色的竹秆上散布着紫色的斑点，宛如泪痕。相传中国历史上的第一个皇帝尧有娥皇、女英两个女儿，姐妹俩同时嫁给继承皇位的舜帝为妃。舜帝驾崩后，失去丈夫的姐妹俩昼夜啼哭，泣泪成血，洒到竹子上，长出来的竹子布满了斑点，从此人们便把它叫做“斑竹”。

·龟甲竹

·斑竹

The Bamboo Viewing Zone

Bamboo is the essence and soul of Ge Garden. In 1998, to the north of Four Seasons Rockeries, Ge Garden had its Bamboo Viewing Zone built with the emphasis on restoring its original appearance of "hundreds types of bamboo and thousands of bamboos". Now, Ge Garden with an area of 12,000 square meters houses more than 60 types of bamboo and nearly 20,000 bamboos total.

As you enter Ge Garden from the north gate on the Yanfu East Road, what comes into sight is thousands of tall slim bamboos piercing into the sky. Those groves of bamboos look like well trained phalanxes of soldiers and their horses in that they remain still in windless weather, and they surge back and forth with the waves of wind. They convey a sense of vigor and prosperity. The bamboo groves of different shapes, dotted with ponds and pavilions, are roughly divided into four parts: Bamboo Forest on Earth Hill, Bamboo Species Appreciation Zone, Waterside Pavilions Mirrored in Clear Stream and Scenic Spot of Western Bamboo.

The name of each bamboo shows its unique features. The Tortoise Shell Bamboo stands out from the other varieties of bamboo in the garden, because it has solid and rough internodes resembling those of a tortoise shell or a dragon's scales; the internodes alternatively face each other on either side. This kind of bamboo is one of the strongest and grows rigidly upright. Compared with other delicate and graceful bamboos, the Tortoise Shell Bamboo looks less tender; however, it has a tougher and hardier bearing.

The Spotted Bamboo, also known in Chinese as Xiangfei Bamboo, is a type of bamboo with stems mottled by dark spots that strike resemblance to teardrops. In Chinese mythology, Emperor Yao, the first emperor in Chinese history, passed his throne down to Emperor Shun and married his two daughters Ehuang and Nvying to him. Later, their beloved husband Shun drowned in the Xiang River. Upon hearing the bad news, Ehuang and Nvying were heartbroken. Leaning on the bamboo, they cried bitterly day and night. Their tears fell all over the surrounding bamboos and stained them forever. Later, the bamboos growing by the Xiang River were all covered with patterns like teardrops. People call such mottled bamboo Xiangfei Bamboo to reminisce the two devoted wives and their love and loyalty.

金镶玉竹、玉镶金竹是园内最多的竹子，此竹色彩美丽，叶片披针形，为优良的观赏竹种。竹秆金黄色，节间带有绿色条纹的是黄金间碧玉；竹秆碧绿色，节间是黄色条纹的即为碧玉间黄金。

慈孝竹又称“孝顺竹”，丛生竹种，笋期在夏季。新笋紧靠老竹，像是遵从古训“父母在，不远游”。而老竹，则殷殷呵护、扶持着新竹免遭风雨侵袭，平安成长。

· 金镶玉竹

· 慈孝竹

The Golden Crook-stem Bamboo and the Yellow Groove Bamboo are the two largest groups in Ge Garden. They are brightly colored, with lance-shaped leaves, making them really outstanding. The Golden Crook-stem Bamboo has tall gleaming-yellow canes with green stripes, while the Yellow Groove Bamboo has smooth bright green canes with yellow stripes.

Bambusa Multiplex, also known as Cixiao Bamboo or Xiaoshun Bamboo, is a tropical bamboo with a clumping habit. Unusually enough, its shooting season falls on summer instead of spring. The new bamboo shoots are nestling near the fully-grown bamboos, which reminds tourists of an old saying "People should not travel far while their parents are still alive." On the other hand, the fully-grown bamboos show their great concern for the newborn bamboos by sheltering them from the wind and rain so that they can grow up, safe and sound.

第三节　何园

何园原名“寄啸山庄”，以东晋著名诗人陶渊明的诗句“倚南窗以寄傲”、“登东皋以舒啸”这一意境命名。由何芷舠在光绪九年（1883年）开始兴建，此园因主人姓何，故人称“何园”。

· 大宅门

何园是扬州保存最完好的古代私家园林，也是全国重点文物保护单位、国家AAAA级旅游景区。何园由东花园、西花园、住宅楼群、片石山房四部分组成，中西合璧、复道回廊是其鲜明特色，因此被园林专家称为“晚清第一园”、“江南园林中的孤例”。

从造园手法看，何园里蕴藏着四个“天下第一”：将后花园分隔为东、西两园的复道回廊被誉为“天下第一廊”；复道回廊上的花窗被称为“天下第一窗”；西花园水池中央的“水心亭”被誉为“天下第一亭”；位于园东南的片石山房被称为“天下第一山”。

东花园

进入何园东大门，迎面一道云墙，遮挡住了园中风景，将游人的目光聚集于墙上的月洞门及门上方的匾额，其隶书“寄啸山庄”为何园主人亲笔所题。东花园景观以厅堂花木为主，疏密有度，重在营造家园的感觉。

一进入东园，呈现在眼前的就是牡丹厅，迎面的山墙上嵌有“凤吹牡丹”的砖雕，图中牡丹枝叶形状有正有反，花纹有疏有密，是砖雕艺术的极

Section Three He Garden

He Garden was originally named Jixiao Villa. This name came from two lines of a poem by Tao Yuanming, a famous poet in the Eastern Jin Dynasty. The two lines read like this: "I lean upon the southern window with immense satisfaction", "I would like to go up Tungkao and make a long-drawn call on the top of the hill." In the 9th year of Emperor Guangxu's reign (1883) in the Qing Dynasty, He Zhidao bought the land and expanded the garden. The garden was then renamed He Garden after the surname of its owner.

He Garden is the best preserved ancient private garden in Yangzhou. It is also an important national-level cultural heritage, as well as a National AAAA Tourist Area. It consists of four parts: the East Garden, the West Garden, the Residential Area, and Pian Shi Shan Fang. The most attractive characteristics of the garden are its double-path corridor and the brilliant combination of Chinese and Western architectural features. It enjoys the reputation of "the most outstanding private garden in the late Qing Dynasty" and "the exceptional case among gardens in South China" among gardening experts.

From the perspective of gardening techniques, He Garden proudly bears four Number Ones. Its covered flyover corridor, which divides the back garden into the eastern and western sections, won the reputation of The Corridor Superior to Elsewhere in the World. The lattice windows in the corridor deserve the title of Number One Windows in the World. The Shuixin Pavilion in the west garden is praised as Number One Pavilion in the World. Pian Shi Shan Fang, which locates in the southeast of He Garden, is extolled as Number One Rockery in the World.

The East Garden

At the east gate of He Garden, what comes into your sight is a cloud-like wall that hides the scenery in the garden, but attracts your attention to the full-moon gate in the wall and its overhead stele, which bears the inscription of "寄啸山庄", written in clerical script by the owner himself. The views in the East Garden mainly consist of halls, flowers and trees arranged in a meticulous style. It aims to create a welcoming atmosphere of home.

When you step into the East Garden, your eyes are drawn to the Peony Hall, with "blowing peony" brick carving patterns on its gable.

· 东门

· "风吹牡丹"砖雕

品。牡丹是何园的园花，牡丹厅周围便是牡丹池，池内种植着牡丹、芍药，花开时节，一片姹紫嫣红。

牡丹厅的北面是一座精致华丽的厅堂——"船厅"。整座厅形似船形，厅周围的地上以鹅卵石、瓦片铺成水波纹状；厅正前方一条方石板铺出的通道好似登船的跳板；低低的台阶，是船的甲板。船厅的抱柱上有对楹联："月做主人梅做客，花为四壁船为家。"何园主人的一生与船有非常密切的联系，其名"芷舠"的含义就是"一只盛着香草的小船"。

· 船厅

· 贴壁假山

东园中最吸引眼球的是北侧的贴壁假山，它如嵌入墙体一般，沿北墙一路攀缘，长达60余米，形成千山万壑、峭壁飞岩的意境。假山上还藏有一条高低盘旋、曲折迂回的山间小道，沿着这条山道经过月亭可登上读书楼，然后与复道回廊联通。

读书楼是何园文脉的象征，当年何家大公子何声灏在这里发愤读书，通过科举，被皇帝钦点为翰林。何氏家族具有厚学重教、诗礼传家的门风，先后出了祖孙翰林、兄弟博士、父女画家、姐弟院士等，玉绣楼何氏家族史料阵列馆内有关于他们故事的记载。

As an invaluable example of the late Qing Dynasty workmanship, the carving impresses visitors with its vivid depiction of both sides of peony branches and leaves, systematic arrangements of floral patterns, and superior craftsmanship. The peony is the garden flower of He Garden, because outside the Peony Hall is a flowerbed containing the Chinese national flower—peony. When in season, varieties of colorful peonies in full bloom create a lovely and beautiful sight.

North of the Peony Hall stands a delicate and magnificent hall named the Ship Hall, because it looks like a ship. The surrounding area is paved with cobblestones, and you may feel as if you were walking on the water. Right in front of the Ship Hall spreads a walkway that is nicely paved with square flagstones. The walkway bears a striking resemblance to a boarding gangway. The low-lying steps are just like the ship's deck. Besides, on the porch of the hall writes a couplet "The ship is a flower-walled house, and it is the place where the moon entertains the plums." He Zhidiao's whole life was closely linked with ships. The most interesting thing is that his first name, "Zhidao", carries the meaning of "a small boat loaded with scented herbs".

The most eye-catching sight in the East Garden is that to the north of the Ship Hall, a rockery leans comfortably against the wall and extends about 60 meters, bringing to mind innumerable mountains and valleys, as well as steep cliffs and lofty rocks. A rugged spiral path winds its way through the rockery. Taking the winding stone steps and passing by the Moon Pavilion, you may find yourself upstairs in the master's Study Building, which is connected with the double-path corridor.

The Study Building is where He Shenghao, the eldest son of He Zhidao, used to spend years studying for a battery of examinations. It symbolizes the He family's tradition of advocating literacy and enhancing their moral values. Owing to his talent and dedication to studies, He Shenghao successively passed the county examination, provincial examination and the Palace examination. Eventually, he was appointed as a member of the Imperial Academy by the emperor. Thanks to the family tradition, the He family cultivated a host of elites: two members of the Imperial Academy (one being He Zhidao's father, the other He Shenghao); two brothers who were awarded Boshi (a kind of official who works in the top university as a professor), namely He Zhidao's two grandsons; two painters; and two academicians. Their stories are written down and displayed in the He Family's Exhibition Hall in the Yuxiu Building.

西花园

如果说东园是后花园的序幕，西园则是后花园的主体。走入西园首先映入眼帘的是贯穿全园的复道回廊，全长1500多米，它是何园中最有特色的建筑，被誉为立交桥的雏型。复道，由双面回廊中间夹一道墙而形成，起到分流的作用。回廊，又称“串楼”，分上下两层，它将东园、西园、住宅院落全都串连在一起。复道分空，回廊曲折，构成了四通八达之利与回环变化之美。回廊的东、南两面墙上开有什锦洞窗和水磨漏窗，形成一道优雅别致的花窗带，是园林花窗中罕见的极品，被推为“花窗之王”。

· 复道

· 回廊

西园以水池居中，池中央一个典雅古朴的方亭便是“水心亭”。这座水心亭是一座保存完好的水中戏亭，专供园主人观赏戏曲、歌舞和纳凉赏景之用。把戏亭建在水上，可以巧妙借助水面与走廊的光影与回声，增强音响与视觉效果。环绕在水池周边的上下楼厅、回廊，便是观戏听曲的最佳场所。

西园北部一座飞檐翘角、气宇不凡的长楼，称为“汇胜楼”。楼上是主人收藏名著典籍、名家字画的地方；楼下有厅堂七间，因厅角昂翘，像振翅欲飞的蝴蝶，故称“蝴蝶厅”，这里是主人宴请宾客的场所。

The West Garden

If the East Garden is compared to the prelude of the back garden, the West Garden is its main body. When you enter the West Garden, what catches your eyes first is its 1,500-meter winding double-path corridor that gives access to the east and west gardens and the houses in the garden. The covered flyover corridor, which is the most distinctive building in He Garden, is appraised as the precursor of the modern overpass in China. Just as the name suggests, it is a double path with one passage above and the other below, and is shaped as a double-sided cloister divided into two by a wall in the middle to divert the flow of visitors. The cloister in the garden, also known as Chuanlou, intersects the whole garden by connecting the upper floors with the lower floors and stringing the two gardens and the buildings together. The two-story winding corridor contributes to the three-dimensional network of passageways leading everywhere and the enchantment of ever changing views when walking along the corridor. Shijin Sculpture Windows and Shuimo Latticed Windows are lined in the east and west walls of the corridor to create a graceful and unique window belt. The lattice windows in the corridor are regarded as rare works of art and appraised as the King of Rosette Windows.

As the key scenic spot of the back garden, the West Garden boasts four different views on the four sides, and contains a pond in its center. In the heart of the pond stands a simple elegant square pavilion called the Shuixin Pavilion. The well-preserved pavilion functions as an overwater the stage for theatrical performances. The He family used to appreciate the Chinese traditional operas and dance performances held here. This also served as a special place for them to enjoy the cool air and scenery. In the construction of the center-pond pavilion, natural elements such as water, echoes and shadows of the corridors are taken into consideration, in order to enhance its sound and visual effects. The upstairs and downstairs balconies and corridors on the four sides of the pond are the ideal places to watch the theatrical performances.

In the north of the West Garden stands the Huisheng Building—a splendid long building with upswept eaves and upturned corners. The owner of the garden used to store his collection of valuable books, paintings and masterpieces of Chinese calligraphy upstairs. The downstairs hall with seven rooms is named the Butterfly Hall because each room has upturned corners that resemble a butterfly flapping its wings. The owner of the garden used to entertain his guests here.

· 水心亭

· 蝴蝶厅

西园水池的西南面有一座湖石假山与水心亭隔水相望。这座湖山体量庞大，奇峰险峭，洞道盘曲，古树名木，苍翠葱郁，呈现了“空山新雨后，天气晚来秋。明月松间照，清泉石上流”的意境。

住宅楼群

从西花园复道曲折南行，可到达一个独立的小楼庭院。这是当年园主人为吃斋念佛、喜欢独处的母亲专门建造的“怡宣楼”。这里是全园赏月的最佳场所，因此又称“赏月楼”。怡萱楼高两层，构造简洁，楼前地面用鹅卵石铺设着“福”、“禄”、“寿”、“喜”图，从法国进口的铁栏杆上刻有“延年益寿”字样。目前，这里已辟为陈列室，展出何氏一族的家谱与有功名祖先的礼服、容像。

穿过怡萱楼的东门，便来到了“玉绣楼”。玉绣楼因院中种植广玉兰和绣球花而得名，其主体建筑是前后各有一座砖木结构的二层小楼，四周以回廊围出院落，无论人在什么位置，从任何一个门出入，都可以沿着回廊绕转一圈，回到原处，这一设计体现了中国传统建筑的串楼理念。同时，玉绣楼的设计又具有鲜明的欧式风格，如百叶窗、壁炉、铁艺床、室内吊灯等，都是当年从西方国家引进的时尚用品。因此，玉绣楼是晚清中国私家园

On the southwest side of the pond is an rock formation made of Taihu stones. It faces the Shuixin Pavilion. With its dramatic peaks and steep cliffs, winding paths, ancient trees, and lush green vegetation, the large-sized rockery recreates the poetic atmosphere of a four-line Tang-dynasty poem, which reads like "In the empty mountain after a fresh rain, the air feels more like autumn at dusk. Bright moon through pines shines, and clear spring over stones flows."

Residential Buildings

Walking southward through the zigzagging double path in the West Garden, you will find yourself standing in a courtyard with a building isolated from the other houses in He Garden. The owner of the garden had the building, namely the Yixuan Building, specially built for his mother, who was a Buddhist and enjoyed solitude. It is the best place in He Garden to appreciate the moon, so it is also called the Moon Appreciation Building. The Yixuan Building is a simple structure with two floors. The ground in front of the building is paved with cobblestones arranged to form the auspicious characters "fortune", "wealth", "longevity" and "happiness". The ironwork fence is carved with four Chinese Characters "延年益寿" that run along the front of the corridor. The front of the corridor was imported from France. The four characters express a wish for longevity. At present, this building has been converted into a showroom to exhibit the He family tree as well as the ceremonial robes and portraits of their famous ancestors.

The east door of the Yixuan Building serves as an entrance to the Yuxiu Building Complex. The building was named after the magnolia and the hydrangea trees growing in the courtyard. The main structure of the Yuxiu Building Complex consists of a front and a back building, each with two floors. The two separate wood-and-brick buildings are joined together by corridors on four sides to form a square courtyard. No matter where you are, or whichever door you choose to come or go through, you can come back to your starting point after touring along the corridor. This is a fine example of the traditional Chinese architecture style of Chuanlou. Meanwhile, the building complex showcases distinctive European style, such as sliding doors, shutters, fireplaces, iron craft beds, and chandeliers. All these fashionable items of that time were imported from abroad. The Yuxiu Building Complex is undoubtedly a typical Chinese private garden of the late Qing Dynasty where the East meets the West, and traditional views and modern concepts are skilfully intertwined. In the corridor

林中东西方两种文化、传统与新潮两种观念相互交融的典型代表。玉绣楼东西两侧的廊道地板上，留有六个直径为38厘米的圆孔，周边用木条围成井栏形状，这是留给佣人从楼下向楼上递送饭菜和物品所用的通道。

· 玉绣楼

从玉绣楼出来，穿过复道回廊东南端的门就进入了“骑马楼”。骑马楼是何园的客舍。骑马，意味着异乡和旅途。当年，国画大师黄宾虹就是在这里度过了一段让他终生难忘的客居时光，并成为何芷舠长孙何适斋与曾孙女何怡如的国画老师。从外形看，骑马楼为东西两幢楼，形似马鞍。其中的东楼亦称东一楼，往北整齐排列东二楼、东三楼。此三幢楼，皆为两层，前后相连，上下相通，宛若迷宫。

· 骑马楼

玉绣楼南面是一座面积为160平方米的“与归堂”，此处为主人会客的地方，是扬州保存最大、最完整的一座楠木厅。与归堂融合了西方建筑的手法，高大庄重的梁柱构架，配以通透华丽的玻璃墙面，一扫中式厅堂的封闭与沉闷，展现了明快敞亮的建筑风格。

片石山房

片石山房位于何园的东南部，原名“双槐园”，始建于清乾隆年间，后被何芷舠购买，相传该园为清初画坛巨匠石涛和尚的叠石孤本。

floors of the west wing and the east wing of the building complex, you can see six round holes, 38cm in diameter. Just as the curbs used in wells, the holes are surrounded by wooden fences. Amazingly, they were used to serve as convenient passages between upstairs and downstairs for raising or lowering dishes and other items.

Exiting the Yuxiu Building Complex and walking through the southeast door of the double-path corridor, you will be led to the Horse Riding Building Complex, the guest house in the garden. Riding on horseback in Chinese means away from home and starting out on a journey. Huang Binhong, an outstanding master of traditional Chinese painting, took up temporary residence in the Horse Riding Building each time he visited Yangzhou. He spent many memorable years here. During his stay in Yangzhou, he was the painting teacher of He Shizhai and He Yiru, who were He Zhidao's eldest grandson and great-granddaughter. The Horse Riding Building Complex, composed of the east building and the west building, looks like a saddle. The two-story east building is also named East Building No.1, because adjacent to the north side are two more two-story buildings, consecutively named East Building No.2 and East Building No.3. The three buildings are a real labyrinth, in which they are connected to each other though passages going back and forth, up and down.

The Yugui Hall (meaning living a secluded and peaceful life) covers an area of 160 square meters and is located in the south of the Yuxiu Building Complex. This magnificent hall, which used to be the place where the owner entertained his guests, is the biggest and best-preserved Nanmu hall in Yangzhou. The western style is also incorporated in the construction of the hall, including the grand lofty post-and-beam framework and walls with stained glass ornaments. These western accents free the hall from the isolation and dullness of a traditional Chinese hall, and enable visitors to enjoy liveliness and spaciousness.

Pian Shi Shan Fang

Pian Shi Shan Fang, initially named Shuang Huai Garden, is located in the southeast of He Garden. It was originally built during the reign of Qianlong in the Qing Dynasty and was later purchased by He Zhidao. The Pian Shi Shan Fang Rockery is said to be the only existing case of the stonework of Shi Tao, a Buddhist monk and a great painting master in the early Qing Dynasty.

片石山房于1989年复修，门额上的“片石山房”是移用石涛墨迹。进入片石山房，门厅天井有“一滴泉”，形成了“注雨观瀑”的景观，让人感到这座小花园的幽雅韵味。

片石山房的园中有一水池贯通南北，池南岸有水榭三间，这里别出心裁地布置了琴棋书画四景。中室引水为泉，时而叮咚，时而铮铮，琴也；东室有古槐树根做的棋台，楚河汉界，棋也；西室有半壁书屋，开卷泼墨，书也；东室南面墙壁上有竹石图窗景，画也。

水池北面的大型湖石假山，即为园林中“天下第一山”，是何园的“镇园之宝”。假山西首为主峰，高约10米，奇峰险俊。山腹藏石室两间，即所谓“片石山房”。石室东西各有洞门出入，盛夏酷暑，烈日炎炎，是消暑的好去处。山势逶迤婉转，走向东南，东南山下筑有石洞与曲桥，山间小道与南部房屋相连，曲折幽深，浑然天成。

· 片石山房

片石山房西边廊壁间嵌有一面大大的玻璃镜，无论从哪个角度看，这面镜子均能将园中景色收入。与镜子遥遥相对的，是东部湖石山下的水池中藏有的一轮“人造月亮”，它随着人行步移，从满月到月牙，逐渐变幻，令人称奇。这两处景点合起来，便是著名而奇特的佛理景观“镜花水月”。

Pian Shi Shan Fang was restored in 1989. The four Chinese characters for "Pian Shi Shan Fang" on the top of the lintel were selected from Shi Tao's original script and made up into what it looks like today. The stream at the foyer reminds the visitors of a spraying waterfall and creates an atmosphere of peace and elegance that permeates in this small exquisite garden.

A pond runs from south to north through Pian Shi Shan Fang. South of the pond are three waterside pavilions, where the settings for lyre-playing, chess, calligraphy and painting are ingeniously laid out and constructed. The middle pavilion stimulates a sense of beauty with the purling water music and the murmuring spring; this is called Lyre-playing. In the east pavilion a chessboard is carved on the root of a locust tree; this is called Chess. The west pavilion, a perfect place to read books and practise calligraphy, attracts the visitors with a good book collection; this is called Calligraphy. A picture of bamboos and stones on its south wall adds to the atmosphere; this is called Painting.

On the north side of the pond is rockwork made of Taihu stones, Number One Rockery in the world. This rockery is one of the four Number Ones in He Garden and also the Treasure of He garden. The west end of the rockwork points to the sky with a peak of about 10 meters. Two stone rooms are hidden in the hillside, hence the name Pian Shi Shan Fang, which means a stone-laid rockery and stone house. The stone house can be entered either through the east or west door. When the summer heat approaches, the stone house is a perfect place to enjoy coolness. The rockery winds its way down to the southeast. At the foot of its southeast hill are some stone caves and a zigzag bridge. A winding path on the hillside is connected to the houses in the south. This stone-laid rockery is indeed a marvelous creation.

In the garden of Pian Shi Shan Fang, a big mirror is built into the wall of its west corridor. The entire garden can be seen in the mirror no matter where the visitor is. East of the rockery, a man-made moon is reflected on the pool water. The mirror and "the man-made moon" stand far apart, facing each other. As the visitors walk along the pool, they will be amazed to watch the gradual changes in the appearance of the moon, from a full moon to a crescent. The mirror and the pool serve the purpose of absorbing the outside scenery, thus turning the real world into a virtual world. This way, a famous and distinctive sight in Buddhist philosophy is achieved here—Flower in the mirror, moon on the water.

第三章
古迹寻踪

在世界运河类遗产中，我国大运河的价值被公认居于首位。扬州处在长江和大运河交汇之处，是名副其实的运河城。大运河和它所衍生的扬州古城，是我国宝贵的历史文化遗产。2007年9月，扬州成为中国大运河申请世界文化遗产牵头城市，大运河申遗的工作正式启动。

扬州城是一座有着2500年历史的古城。国家发展和改革委员会公布的国家100处大遗址名单中，江苏仅两处上榜，扬州古城遗址（隋-宋）便是其中之一，这是扬州的骄傲！扬州古城遗址申请世界文化遗产工作，也已经于2006年6月启动。

扬州古城内古街名宅、古刹名寺、古祠古墓众多，有着丰富的历史内涵和极高的文化价值，近年来得到了充分的保护和利用。

Chapter III

Traces of Ancient Historical Relics

On the world list of Canal Heritage, the Grand Canal in China has long been recognized as the most valuable. Located at the junction of the Yangtze River and the Grand Canal, Yangzhou, a canal city worthy of its name, has become a valuable historical and cultural heritage in China. In September 2007, Yangzhou became the first city on the Grand Canal to officially apply for the title of World Cultural Heritage Site.

Yangzhou is an ancient city with a history of about 2,500 years. On the list of the 100 large national heritage sites released by the National Development and Reform Commission, only two sites in Jiangsu are included, one of which is the Old Town of Yangzhou from the Sui Dynasty to the Song Dynasty. This is the pride of Yangzhou! What's more, it was in June 2006 that the Old Town of Yangzhou applied for World Cultural Heritage started.

In the city there are numerous ancient streets, houses, temples, ancestral temples and tombs. These ancient landmarks have rich historical significance and extremely high cultural value and have been carefully protected and fully developed in the recent years.

第一节　古运河

·扬州古运河风光带

大运河是扬州的母亲河，扬州城因运河而生、而兴、而盛，也因运河而衰。唐代诗人皮日休对隋炀帝开凿大运河作出了这样的评价：“尽道隋亡为此河，至今千里赖通波。若无水殿龙舟事，共禹论功不较多。”既批判了隋炀帝的奢侈无道，也充分肯定了他开通运河的历史功绩。直至今日，大运河仍然承担着我国北煤南运、南粮北运和南水北调的重任。

1958年，京杭运河扬州临城段改线工程开工，从湾头壁虎坝开挖新河直接往南至六圩长江边。扬州城区段的运河旧道终于安静了许多，成了“古运河”。

现在扬州市区段古运河，从茱萸湾起至瓜洲镇入长江，长约30公里，两岸的历史遗迹星罗棋布，广场和各种主题博物馆景景相连，形成了古运河名胜风光带。

大王庙

·古邗沟畔的大王庙

扬州市区高桥路的北端是黄金坝闸，由该闸往西的东西向河流，便是通向古邗城脚下的邗沟故道。而紧挨在黄金坝闸东北边的，是大王庙广场。大王庙也叫吴王庙，里面供奉的两位大王，一位是春秋时的吴王夫差，一位是西汉初期的吴王刘濞。夫差下令开挖了沟通长江与淮河的古邗沟，并修筑邗城，对扬州的发展有开拓之功；刘濞则长于发展经济，开凿了由茱萸湾向东经泰州到如皋，直达海边的运盐河，将海边生产出来的海盐运往

Section One The Ancient Canal

The Grand Canal is the mother river of Yangzhou. Simultaneous with her, Yangzhou city was built, developed, achieved prosperity, and even went into decline with her decay. Pi Rixiu, a poet of the Tang Dynasty, once made the following comment on Emperor Yang of the Sui Dynasty who had the Grand Canal built: "Everyone complains that the Sui Dynasty ended because of the canal; however, it is still an important way for people to travel. If he hadn't had so many palaces and dragon boats built, his merits could have been compared with Dayu." The poet not only criticized the emperor's dissolute behavior, but also fully recognized his achievements. Nowadays, the Grand Canal still shoulders the responsibilities of transporting coal from the North to the South, transporting grain from the South to the North, and delivering water from the South to the North.

In 1958, the route-conversion project of the canal in the outskirts of Yangzhou was carried out. The excavation of the new channel started from the Lizard Dam in the Wantou town and extended southwards to where the Liuwei town and the Yangtze River meet. The canal in Yangzhou finally became a quiet "ancient canal".

Now the part of the ancient canal in Yangzhou flows from the Mastixia Bay (Zhuyuwan) to the Guazhou town, where it joins the Yangtze River. It is about 30 km in length, dotted with historical sites on both sides. Connected to plazas and a variety of theme museums, the famous scenic spot along the Grand Canal has been created.

The Dawang Temple

On the north end of the Gaoqiao Road in Yangzhou stands the Gold Embankment, with a river flowing from west to east in the old course of the ancient Han Canal. Next to the Gold Embankment in the northeast is the Dawang Temple Square. The Dawang Temple, also known as the King Wu Temple, is dedicated to the two kings, Fu Chai, King of the State of Wu in the Spring and Autumn Period, and Liu Bi, King of the State of Wu in the early Western Han Dynasty. Fu Chai began the pioneering work by ordering the excavation of the ancient Han Canal, connecting the Yangtze River and the Huai River. He also had the Hancheng built. Liu Bi excelled in developing economy. He started the excavation of the salt transport river, which runs eastwards

广陵（今扬州）销售，赚取了大量的钱财，使吴国成为当时经济实力最强的藩国，扬州在历史上第一次进入了繁荣昌盛的时期。刘濞也被扬州人奉为财神，所以大王庙也叫“财神庙”。

茱萸湾

· 茱萸湾

市区东北部的湾头镇，汉代时因盛产茱萸，称茱萸村，吴王刘濞开凿的运盐河也叫茱萸沟，就是在茱萸村与邗沟交汇。隋文帝时期这里更名为茱萸湾。

自隋至清，茱萸湾扼守运河咽喉，成为扬州城的重要门户。漕运、盐运，商贾僧道、迁客骚人、公卿帝王，南来北往多会经停这里。来自海外各国的大量商船与货物也在这里进行交易。历朝历代，古湾头镇几度繁华，而每逢战事发生，这里又成为兵家必争之地。如今，根据政府规划，湾头茱萸古镇古闸历史地段，将维持现存古街道及古街区的原有风貌。

东关古渡

· 东关古渡

自唐代以后，东关古渡一直是扬州城的东大门，运河上帆樯林立，古渡口人声鼎沸。其西侧现建有宋大城东门遗址公园，复建了东关古城门和城楼。城门内便是东关街，在唐代，这里店铺鳞次栉比，人流摩肩接踵，是最繁华的商业街。

明清时代，东关街吸引了众多盐商富贾聚居于此。街旁大小园林密布，其中最有名的是黄至筠的个园、汪懋麟的百尺梧桐阁和马氏兄弟的小玲珑山馆（也称“街南书屋”）。

from the Mastixia Bay far to the sea side via Taizhou and Rugao. Thus, the salt produced at the seaside could be transported to Guangling (the present-day Yangzhou) to be sold. The salt industry made the Sate of Wu the most economically powerful of the vassal states in the Western Han Dynasty; hence Yangzhou came to enjoy prosperity for the first time in her history. As a result, Liu Bi was regarded as God of Wealth by the people of Yangzhou, and the temple is also called the Temple of God of Wealth.

The Mastixia Bay

The Wantou town in the northeast of Yangzhou city was once called the Mastixia village because it was abundant in Mastixia trees during the Han Dynasty. The salt transport river excavated by Liu Bi was also named the Mastixia Canal because the Mastixia village and the ancient Han Canal met here. During the reign of Emperor Wen of the Sui Dynasty, it was renamed the Mastixia Bay.

From the Sui Dynasty to the Qing Dynasty, the Mastixia Bay was the vital gateway of Yangzhou for transportation of grain and salt. Also, many merchants, monks, famous men of letters, senior officials, and even lords and emperors stopped by here. Besides, a large number of merchant ships from overseas traded goods here. Overall, the town of Wantou experienced several prosperous periods. In times of war, however, it was a contested hot spot. Now, according to the government's planning, the historical district of the old Mastixia town will maintain its original appearance.

The Ancient Dongguan Ferry

Ever since the Tang Dynasty, the ancient Dongguan Ferry has been the east gateway to Yangzhou, constantly with a constant hustle and bustle and a thick forest of boats moored on the canal. Together with the old Dongguan city gate and tower, the East Gate Relics Park of Song Dacheng was reconstructed in the west. Inside the gate is the Dongguan Street, which was the most bustling commercial street in the Tang Dynasty, with rows of shops on each side and crowds of people jostling with each other.

During the Ming and Qing Dynasties, the Dongguan Street attracted many salt merchants and wealthy people to live here. As a result, private gardens of various sizes emerged, the most famous of which are Ge Garden rebuilt by Huang Zhijun, the Hundred-

· 普哈丁墓园

普哈丁墓园

自唐宋以后，常有来自阿拉伯和波斯的胡商云集扬州。在东关古渡的南边、运河的东岸有一组伊斯兰风格的建筑，这便是扬州唯一的一处古代外国人的墓葬地，名为“普哈丁墓”，是全国重点文物保护单位。据说普哈丁是伊斯兰教创始人穆罕默德的第十六世裔孙，南宋末年由海上来扬州传教10年，并建造了扬州第一座清真寺——仙鹤寺。后来他去山东传教，在乘船返回扬州时，病逝于船中，后被葬在古运河东岸的土岗上。此后，历代有声望的中外伊斯兰教人士归真后陆续葬在这里，形成了一座墓园。墓园内设有资料陈列室，还有一座清真寺。墓园内有一株高大的银杏树，树龄已有700多年。从这座墓园可以反映出，中国人民和阿拉伯人民的友谊源远流长。

宝塔湾

宝塔湾是古运河的一个转弯处，因旁边的文峰塔而得名。文峰塔建于明代，砖木结构，七层八面，既玲珑又雄伟，是古运河边的一座地标性建筑。

· 文峰塔

古时的宝塔湾是古运河上重要的港口。文峰寺门前不远处的河岸旁，立有一石碑，上书“古运河”三字。碑文说明，鉴真六次东渡，有三次从这里出发，奔向大海。

foot Chinese Parasol Tree Pavilion owned by Wang Maolin and the Ma brothers' Little Translucent Mountain Lodge—also known as the Bookroom on the South Side of the Street.

The Islamic Puhaddin Tomb Park

Since the Tang and Song Dynasties, many merchants from Arabia and Persia have come to Yangzhou for business. South of the Dongguan Ferry, an architectural complex in Islamic style is located along the eastern bank of the Grand Canal. This is the only ancient graveyard for foreigners in Yangzhou, and houses the tomb of Puhaddin. It is also an important national-level cultural heritage. According to the historical records, Puhaddin was the sixteenth generation descendant of the founder of Islam—Mohammed. In the late Southern Song Dynasty he came to Yangzhou by sea for missionary purpose. He spent a total of ten years in Yangzhou, during which he built the first mosque—the Fairy Crane Mosque. Later he went to Shandong to preach Islam and died on a boat during his return to Yangzhou. After his death, he was buried on a hillock on the eastern bank of the Grand Canal. From then on Puhaddin has been respected as a sage by Chinese Muslims. Thereafter, those famous Chinese and foreign Muslims who died would be buried here. In the graveyard there is a display room, a mosque, and a tall 700-year-old ginkgo tree. This graveyard reflects the long-lasting friendship between Chinese and Arabs.

The Pagoda Bay

The Pagoda Bay, named after the Wenfeng Pagoda standing nearby, lies around the curve of the ancient canal. Built in the Ming Dynasty, the seven-story octahedral Wenfeng Pagoda is a brick-and-wood building and still a landmark on the Grand Canal, both exquisite and magnificent.

In ancient times, the Pagoda Bay was an important port on the Grand Canal. On the bank, not far from the Wenfeng Temple, stands a stone tablet with three Chinese characters "古运河". The letters on the monument tell visitors that Master Jian Zhen sailed to Japan six times to preach Buddhism. Three times he set out from here and traveled east to Japan by sea.

三汊河

古运河流到扬州城南十多里处，河流分成两支，一支向南由瓜洲入长江，一支向西由仪征入长江，因而民间把这里称做“三汊河”。古时候，由苏南、浙江去北方的船只都是经镇江、瓜洲来扬州，而自湖北、湖南、江西、安徽出发去北方的船只多是从仪征至三汊河来扬州。两条水道在三汊河汇流。在这样一处风水宝地，矗立着巍峨壮丽的禅宗名刹高旻寺。康熙、乾隆南巡时多次暂住的塔湾行宫也修建在这里。

瓜洲古渡

瓜洲渡口位于波平浪缓的古运河与急流奔涌的长江衔接处。“汴水流，泗水流，流到瓜洲古渡头，吴山点点愁”（白居易），“京口瓜洲一水间，钟山只隔数重山”（王安石），“楼船夜雪瓜洲渡，铁马秋风大散关”（陆游），这些脍炙人口的诗篇描述了瓜洲引人入胜的景观。唐代扬州人张若虚的《春江花月夜》，写出了瓜洲古渡月色朦胧、清流平缓的奇景。古代剧作家将《杜十娘怒沉百宝箱》的场景也安排在这里。

· 瓜洲古渡

古时候，瓜洲一直是交通要津和江防要地，建有城池和许多亭台楼阁，历来为兵家所争。康熙、乾隆两位皇帝每次南巡都曾下榻设在瓜洲的行宫。

根据政府规划，瓜洲古镇江口后街历史地段，将注重维持现存古街区及古街道的原有风貌。

The Sancha River

The ancient canal is divided into two branches, one flowing south into the Yangtze River via Guazhou and the other flowing west to the Yangtze River via Yizheng. Therefore people call it the Sancha River, meaning three braided rivers. In ancient times, ships from South of Jiangsu or Zhejiang would pass through Yangzhou via Zhenjiang and Guazhou and then head north, while ships from Hubei, Hunan, Jiangxi and Anhui would pass through Yangzhou through Yizheng and the Sancha River and then head north. The two channels join in the Sancha River. In such a favored place stands a famous majestic Zen temple—the Gaomin Monastery. Each time Emperors Kangxi and Qianlong toured the South, they visited Yangzhou. For their stay in Yangzhou, the travel lodge was built in the Gaomin Monastery.

The Ancient Guazhou Ferry

The ancient Guazhou Ferry is located where the ancient canal and the Yangtze River meet. The following are some famous ancient poems eulogizing the Guazhou Ferry.

Waters of Bian flow,
Waters of Si flow,
Flow to the old ferry of Guazhou,
The hills in Wu bow in sorrow. (Bai Juyi)
Between Jingkou and Guazhou a sole river lies,
Zhongshan will be soon in sight after a few hills. (Wang Anshi)
In the autumn wind the war horses are standing in an impregnable pass,
Whereas on a snowy night the war ships are waiting in the Guazhou Ferry. (Lu You)

Moonlight on the Spring River by Zhang Ruoxu, a Yangzhou citizen in the Tang Dynasty, described the beautiful scenery of Guazhou of the dim moonlight with gently flowing river. The background of the drama *Du Shiniang Sank the Treasure Chest in Anger* was also set here.

In ancient times, many cities, pavilions, and terraces of strategic importance in terms of transportation and defense were built near the Guazhou Ferry. Apart from that, Emperors Kangxi and Qianlong also had a travel lodge built here for their southern tours.

According to the government's planning, every effort will be made to maintain the original style of the ancient neighborhoods and streets in the old town of Guazhou.

第二节　古城遗址

历史上，扬州城屡毁屡建，城区位置与范围也几经更迭。在扬州市区保障湖北边的土岗上，有个堡城村，这里便是宋朝以前古扬州城的城址所在地。城址四周的城墙、城壕仍然较为清晰完整。村中有一个不起眼的院落，是唐代扬州大都督府以及淮南节度使衙署所在地。

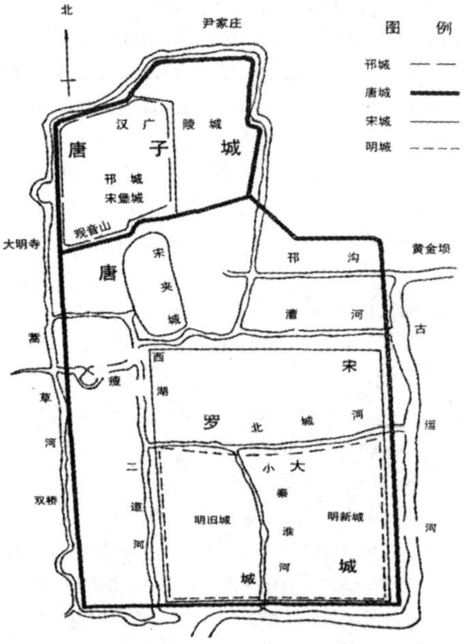

· 扬州古城址变迁图

春秋时代的邗城

春秋时期的邗城是最早的扬州城。邗城呈方形，城墙用土夯筑而成，周长约10里。南城墙建在蜀岗南侧的断崖上。传说城没有南门，北城墙上也仅有一水门，只有东西城墙上设有城门。邗城当时离长江并不远，原为战争而筑，供屯军、储粮或督运之用，为吴国的军事行动提供后勤保障。

战国时期，公元前319年，楚国在邗城旧址上重筑新城，取名为“广陵城”。

汉代的广陵城

刘邦平定淮南王英布的叛乱后，封其侄刘濞为吴王，领三郡五十三县，国都设在广陵。刘濞在吴国境内大力发展经济，广陵的商业很繁荣。刘濞先在原楚国广陵城的城址上建内城，又在内城以东建东郭城，使得扩建后的广陵城周长达到14.5里。

自西汉重筑广陵城以后，该城历经东汉、魏晋、南朝，直到隋代，城池虽有兴废，但城址未变，地下的文化遗存应该是十分丰富的。

Section Two Ruins of the Ancient City

Throughout history, Yangzhou city was destroyed and rebuilt several times. Its urban areas also experienced many changes. On the hummock north of the Baozhang Lake lies the Baocheng village. It was the site of the ancient Yangzhou before the Song Dynasty, with the outline of the ancient city walls and moats clearly seen. In a humble courtyard of the village lies the former site of the Yangzhou Grand Military Government and the Military Commissioner's Office of Huainan of the Tang Dynasty.

The Hancheng in the Spring and Autumn Period

The Hancheng in the Spring and Autumn Period is the precursor of the present-day city of Yangzhou. It was square with an earthen city wall approximately ten *li* in circumference. The south city wall was erected on top of the Shugang Ridge. According to the legend, there were gates in the east and west walls, a water gate in the north wall, but no gate in the south wall. The Hancheng then was not far from the Yangtze River, because it was originally built to facilitate the transport of troops and provisions when the State of Wu had conflicts with its rivals.

During the Warring States Period, the State of Chu built a new city on the former site of the Hancheng in 319 BC and named it Guangling, meaning "wide tumulus".

The Guangling City in the Han Dynasty

After suppressing the rebellion of Ying Bu, King of Huainan (a prefecture-level city), Liu Bang appointed his nephew Liu Bi as the King of the State of Wu to govern three prefectures and fifty-three counties. The Guangling city was made the capital of the State of Wu. Liu Bi not only devoted major efforts to developing the economy, but also expanded the city. First, he had the inner city built on the former site of Guangling and then the Dongguo city east of the inner city. After the extension, the city wall of Guangling measured approximately fourteen and a half *li* in circumference (a little over five miles).

Since the rebuilding in the Western Han Dynasty, the Guangling city experienced several ups and downs throughout the Eastern Han Dynasty, the Wei and Jin Dynasties, the Southern Dynasty, and the Sui Dynasty. However, since the city site basically remained unchanged in those successive dynasties, the underground cultural relics are presumably as diverse as they are abundant.

唐代的衙城和罗城

扬州唐城遗址博物馆位于大明寺东侧不远处，建在唐衙城遗址的西南角。该博物馆建于1989年，馆内展出了扬州出土的唐代文物，分别从城池与行政区域、手工业与商业、文化艺术、对外往来等方面，直观地展示了唐代扬州的繁华景象。

· 扬州唐城博物馆

唐代的扬州，由于运河的通畅、经济的繁荣和人口的增多，城市规模大为扩展，城池由两部分组成。坐落在蜀岗之上的是“子城”，也称“牙城”或“衙城”，聚集着众多的官衙、府署，面积约3平方千米。这里也是原先隋炀帝的宫城所在，它的范围与汉代广陵城大体一致。坐落在蜀岗之南的叫“罗城”，是在滨江平原上另建的新城。这里居民集中，街道整齐，店铺林立，商业繁荣。

由众多专家组成的扬州唐城考古队，经过多年的勘探和发掘，解开了罗城之谜，绘出了扬州唐城平面图。罗城呈长方形，它北起保障湖和竹西中学北侧的平山堂东路，南至南通路和扬州大学主楼一线，东起泰州路、高桥路和黄金坝路，西至市中医院西侧的宝带河，以及瘦西湖万花园西侧水道。罗城南城墙上的正门位于现在的南门遗址广场。现在城北鸿福一村北侧的狭长空地，就是罗城北城墙所在的位置。罗城已钻探出七座城门和一个水门遗址。罗城内多次挖掘出较大的手工作坊遗迹，出土文物上千件，说明扬州当时的手工业很发达。

The Yacheng and the Luocheng in the Tang Dynasty

The Museum of the Ruins of Yangzhou City in the Tang Dynasty is located to the east of the Daming Temple, in the southwest corner of the former site of the Tang Yacheng. Founded in 1989, the museum displays the Tang Dynasty's cultural relics unearthed in Yangzhou, demonstrating great prosperity of Yangzhou in the Tang Dynasty from different aspects, such as the city and its districts, handicraft and commerce, arts and culture, foreign trade and external exchange and so on.

In the Tang Dynasty, due to the smooth transport along the Grand Canal, rapid growth in population, and economic prosperity, Yangzhou city expanded greatly and was divided into two parts. Located on the Shugang Ridge is the Zicheng (also called Yacheng) where a large number of administrative headquarters and offices were concentrated, covering an area of about 3 square kilometers. It was also the former site of the residential palace of Emperor Yang in the Sui Dynasty, and its size was approximately the same as the Guangling city in the Han Dynasty. The Luocheng in the south of the Shugang Ridge was a new city built on plains not far from the ocean, where the newly-populated districts enjoyed a well-planned layout of tidy streets, numerous shops, and a prosperous economy.

The myth of the Luocheng was unveiled by the Archaeological Team of Yangzhou Tang City. After many years of explorations and excavations, the team experts worked out a layout map of Yangzhou city in the Tang Dynasty. The Luocheng had a rectangular shape, bordering the Baozhang Lake and the Pingshan Hall East Road (north of Zhuxi Middle School) in the north; the Nantong Road and the main building of Yangzhou University in the south; the Taizhou Road, the Gaoqiao Road, and the Gold Embankment Road in the east; the Bao Dai River (west of Yangzhou Chinese Traditional Medicine Hospital) and the water way west of the Multicolored Garden of the Slender West Lake Scenic Spot in the west. The front gate of the south city wall lies in the present-day Southern Gate Relics Plaza. The long and narrow space on the north side of Hongfu Yicun is the original location of the north city wall of the Luocheng. Seven gates and a site of a water gate of the Luocheng have been revealed. Archaeological excavations in the Luocheng have unearthed several sites of large-scale handcraft workshops and over 1,000 antiques, illustrating that Yangzhou's handcraft industry was well developed at that time.

子城和罗城上下相连，所以被称为两重城。两重城南北长6030米，东西最宽处为3120米，整个城的面积约有18平方千米，其规模在当时仅次于长安和洛阳。运河水系与城内水系浑然一体，城内外河道纵横，桥梁众多，码头绵延，帆樯林立，船只之多大大超过车马。

宋代的扬州三城

南宋时期，扬州成了江淮地区抗金、抗元的前线，所修城池较为坚固，该城史称“宋大城”。宋大城南墙和东墙沿用唐代罗城的南墙和东墙；西城墙的位置在今双虹桥、石塔桥、大虹桥、长春桥一线东侧；北城墙在现在的漕河路一线。宋大城全部用大砖砌造，东西南北四个城门均建有翁城，北门侧边还设有水门，这在各地的城池结构中非常罕见。

· 宋大城东门城楼

后来，为适应军事需要，又在蜀岗唐代的子城废墟上筑城，称为“堡城”。堡城与宋大城南北相对，中间相隔约一公里，于是又筑“夹城”连接二者，以通往来。所以当时扬州一地有三城，即宋大城、堡城和夹城，总称“宋三城”。因夹城形似蜂腰，所以又称宋三城为“蜂腰城”。

· 宋夹城城楼

现在，宋代的堡城保存比较完整，除极少部分城墙被破坏外，绝大部分夯土城墙均高出地面，四面的护城河仍在，里面或长着莲藕，或种着水芹。在宋夹城则复建了部分古城门和

The outer city, also known as the Luocheng, was connected to the inner city, known as the Zicheng. Therefore, Yangzhou city in the Tang Dynasty is also called the Dual City. The city walls run 6,030 meters from north to south, measuring 3,120 meters from east to west at the widest point. Covering a total land area of about 18 square kilometers, Yangzhou city in the Tang Dynasty was second only to Chang'an and Luoyang. The water system within the city and that of the canal intertwined naturally. With countless bridges over the water, numerous docks along the banks and great numbers of junks stretching for miles and miles, the waterways intersect like a spider web inside and outside the city. Therefore, it was not unusual to see more boats than horse-drawn carriages during that time in Yangzhou.

The Triple City of Yangzhou in the Song Dynasty

During the Southern Song Dynasty, Yangzhou became the front line in the Jianghuai area, fighting against the Jin and Yuan invaders, therefore the city was strong and sturdy in construction. It was known as Song Dacheng in history. The south and east walls of the Luocheng in the Tang Dynasty were reused as the south and east walls of Song Dacheng. The west wall was located on the east side of the present-day Shuanghong Bridge, the Shita Bridge, the Great Rainbow Bridge, and the Changchun Bridge. The north wall ran along the present-day Cao River Road. Song Dacheng was built completely with large bricks, with a Wengcheng on the east, west, south, and north gates. Water gates were built on both sides of the north gate, which was very rare in the layouts of cities.

Later, for military purposes, the Garrison City (Baocheng) was founded on the former site of the Zicheng on the Shugang Ridge. There was about one kilometer between the Baocheng in the north and Song Dacheng in the south. Therefore, another bastion called the Jiacheng was built to link the Baocheng with Song Dacheng. The Baocheng, the Jiacheng and Song Dacheng made Yangzhou a complex triple city in the Southern Song Dynasty, hence its name Song Sancheng. Besides, the Jiacheng resembled a wasp waist, bringing another name for Song Sancheng—Wasp Waist City.

Now, the Baocheng of the Song Dynasty is relatively well preserved, except for some parts of the walls. For the most part, the earth-ridged town walls tower above the ground, surrounded by a moat, with lotus flowers and water celery growing inside. In the Jiacheng, parts of the

城楼，四面宽阔的护城河也被全部打通，已建设成为湿地公园，供市民和游客休憩游览。

宋大城西门遗址博物馆在今四望亭路旁，这里发现了五代、北宋、南宋、明、清五个朝代的西门遗址，各个时代的城墙基础、砖铺路面的地层叠压关系极为清晰，在我国相当罕见。宋大城东门遗址在今东关街东口。宋大城北门遗址在今漕河西路与凤凰桥街交叉处，今已建成北门遗址广场。扬州城南门遗址广场在今南门街南口。在这些地方，人们可以领略到扬州古城的雄浑风采和沧桑变迁。

明清时代的扬州城

元朝时候，宋大城只剩下一部分。元末农民战争中，宋大城更是损毁严重，城中曾经仅剩18户人家。

明朝初年，扬州城开始得到恢复，先是在原宋大城的西南角修筑一小城，该城西起扬州中学西围墙、扬州大学附属中学西部边缘，东至小秦淮河边，南墙与唐罗城南墙一致，北墙在今盐阜路一线。小城有五个城门，其中西为通泗门，东为大东门和小东门。南北还各有一个水门，引官河水流贯城中，称为市河，即后来的汶河。这就是明代的扬州“旧城”。

明嘉靖年间，为防倭寇入侵，在旧城东廓外建一外城。外城东墙和南墙与唐代罗城东墙、南墙位置相同，北墙在今盐阜路一线，这就是明代的扬州“新城”。新城与旧城之间虽隔有城墙和小秦淮河，但两城相连，实为一体。

ancient city gates and towers were restored; also, the wide moat was dredged, allowing the water to flow freely around the city. Now, a wetland park has been created here so that the citizens and visitors can enjoy a relaxing and peaceful atmosphere.

The Song Dacheng Museum of the West Gates Ruins is located on the Siwangting Road. Here, the archaeological excavations unearthed the ruins of the respective west gates in the Five Dynasties, Northern Song, Southern Song, Ming and Qing Dynasties. The city wall foundations and layers of brick-paved roads for each dynasty are clearly shown, which is a very rare case in China. The site of Song Dacheng East Gate is at the east end of present Dongguan Street. At the junction of the Cao River Road and the Phoenix Bridge Street lies the site of Song Dacheng North Gate, where the North Gate Ruins Plaza has been built. The South Gate Ruins Plaza is at the south end of the South Gate Street. These historical and cultural relics display the grandeur of the ancient Yangzhou and illustrate the vicissitudes in the city's fortunes.

Yangzhou City in the Ming and Qing Dynasties

During the Yuan Dynasty, only a part of Song Dacheng survived. Wars of the late Yuan Dynasty drastically reduced the population to only 18 families. The whole town was almost ruined.

Yangzhou began to recover in the early Ming Dynasty. First, on the southwest corner of the site of Song Dacheng, a small town was built. Its west city wall extended from the west wall of Yangzhou High School to the west of the High School Affiliated with Yangzhou University. The Small Qinhuai River was in its east end. The south city wall was that of the Luocheng of the Tang Dynasty, while its north wall used to stand along the Yanfu Road. The town had five gates, the Tongsi Gate in the west as well as the Big East Gate and the Small East Gate in the east. Both the south wall and the north wall were equipped with water gates, through which the water of the Guan River (later known as the Wen River) was diverted into the town. This was the Old Town in the Ming Dynasty.

During the reign of Jiajing in the Ming Dynasty, an outer city to the east of the Old Town was built to protect the town from pirates' invasions. The east and south walls of the outer city lied in those of the Luocheng, while its north wall ran along the Yanfu Road. This was the New Town of Yangzhou. The New Town was separated from the Old Town by the city wall and the Small Qinhuai River, which ensured the continuity and integrity of the two towns.

清代及民国均沿用明代城池。1951年，古老的城墙被拆除，在其基础上筑起了南通路、盐阜路、泰州路，连同之前修的淮海路，形成扬州第一道环城马路。

· 文昌阁

文昌阁是明代建筑，外形优美，很早就被当作了扬州城的城标。现在的汶河路在唐代是扬州城内的一条河。1959年填汶河筑路，命名为“汶河路”。文昌阁其实是建造在汶河上的一座桥上，而这座桥半个多世纪前在填河时被埋入了地下。

When it came to the Qing Dynasty and the Republic of China, Yangzhou city retained its appearance in the Ming Dynasty. In 1951, the old city walls were demolished and instead, the Nantong Road, the Yanfu Road, and the Taizhou Road were constructed, reaching the previously-built Huaihai Road and forming the first ring road of Yangzhou.

Built in the Ming Dynasty, the Wenchang Pavilion bears a distinct architectural style of that time. With its beautiful appearance, it has been regarded as the symbol of Yangzhou. The present-day Wenhe Road used to be a river in Yangzhou city in the Tang Dynasty. In 1959, the Wenhe River was filled in and converted to the Wenhe Road. The Wenchang Pavilion used to be a pavilion built on a bridge over the Wenhe River, but more than half a century ago the bridge was buried underground when the river was filled in.

第三节　古街名宅

在扬州老城区，老街古巷密布，有近600条，并深藏着大大小小几十座宅第园林。这里的青石方砖、高高的风火墙、砖雕门楼、深宅大院，无不散发着浓郁的历史气息。目前，扬州老城区的保护与利用，将以东关街、仁丰里、湾子街和南河下四个历史文化街区为重点，以保持扬州老城区的传统风貌与特色。

东关街历史文化街区

该街区即通常所说的“双东”地区，双东即指东关街与东圈门。这里传统的商业市井气息、深厚的历史文化氛围，都是保护的重点。街区内有老字号建筑17处，名人故居15处。

·东关街

东关街是扬州遗留下来的惟一一条唐代古街。古街西部的逸圃东邻个园，为民国初年银行家李鹤生所筑。过去，扬州市国画院曾设在逸圃办公。近年，逸圃全貌得到了恢复，并被列为江苏省文物保护单位。跟逸圃隔街相望的，是清朝直隶提督李长乐的宅第，建于同治年间。李宅现已整修一新，命名为“长乐客栈”，作为高档旅游酒店接待游客。

位于个园南侧、正处于大规模复建中的街南书屋，原是清代盐业巨子、时人称“扬州二马”的儒商马曰琯、马曰璐兄弟俩的宅第与园林。当时马氏藏书十万卷，文采风流，乐善好施，蜚声全国。街南书屋的东边，已部分复建并对外开放的“馥园”，是在原谢馥春旧址上改建的。“谢馥春”是中国第一家化妆品企业的名号，距今已有182年的历史。

·东圈门

Section Three Ancient Streets and Houses

In the old town of Yangzhou, there are nearly 600 ancient streets, dozens of mansions and gardens of different sizes. Here, the cordierite bricks, high fire walls, carved bricks and gatehouses, as well as grand mansions with spacious courtyards all bear profound historical flavor. At present, to preserve its traditional features and characteristics, the old town of Yangzhou emphasizes protection and utilization of the following four historical and cultural areas: the Dongguan Street, Renfengli, the Wanzi Street, and Nanhexia.

The Historic District of the Dongguan Street

This district is known as the Double East Area, namely the Dongguan Street and the Dongquan Gate. The focus of the protection efforts is on preserving the traditional business atmosphere as well as the rich historical and cultural atmosphere. There remain 17 old buildings and 15 former residences of celebrities.

The Dongguan Street is the only ancient street survived from the Tang Dynasty in Yangzhou. To the west of the street and to the east of Ge Garden is the Yipu Garden, which was built by the banker Li Hesheng in the early years of the Republic of China. Yangzhou Traditional Chinese Painting Academy used to have its offices here. In the recent years, the Yipu Garden has been restored, and has become a cultural heritage under protection of Jiangsu Province. Across the street is the mansion of Li Changle, who was the prefect of the Zhili area (present-day Hebei Province) in the early years of the Emperor Tongzhi in the Qing Dynasty. Now the mansion has been remodeled into a high-level tourism hotel called Changle Hotel.

Located on the south side of Ge Garden, the Bookroom on the South Side of the Street is under repair. It was originally the mansion and garden of two brothers—scholars and businessmen Ma Yueguan and Ma Yuelu, known as the salt industry tycoons in the Qing Dynasty or the Two Mas of Yangzhou. At that time they had a book collection of over one hundred thousand volumes. They were famous throughout the country for erudite knowledge and willingness to help others. East of the Bookroom on the South Side of the Street is the Fuyuan Garden, which has been partly rebuilt and open to the public. Actually, it was rebuilt on the original site of Xiefuchun, the first Chinese cosmetic brand with a history of 182 years.

东圈门街附近文物古迹众多，如“青溪旧屋”，是清代扬州学派重要代表之一刘文淇的住宅。当然最为著名的还是省级文物保护单位——汪氏小苑。

汪氏小苑

汪氏小苑是扬州现存最为完整的清末民初盐商住宅之一。

苑内住宅横为三路并列，纵为主房三进延伸，前后中轴贯穿，左右两厢对称，体现着中国儒家的中庸思想。住宅庭院比例均衡，通风采光充足，纵横互相联通，内外分合自如，是扬州大宅门传统格局形式之一。厅前屋后辟“可栖”、“小苑春深”、“迎曦”三处玲珑精巧的小花园，使住宅与园林揉为一体，曲折多变。

· 小苑春深

住宅内木雕、砖雕、石雕与墙面、地面巧妙结合，浑然一体。雕刻取材珍贵，技法多样，题材丰富，寓意深刻。

仁丰里历史文化街区

仁丰里是位于汶河路以东，国庆路以西的一条南北向的古街。该街区东至小秦淮河，南至曹李巷一线，西至迎春巷、史巷，北至旧城七巷。

街区内的毓贤街6-8号住宅，是清代扬州学派代表、封疆大吏阮元的故居。紧挨在阮元故居东南边的，便是老城区有名的佛寺——旌忠寺。

In the Dongquan Gate Historical Area there are a number of cultural heritages, for example, the Green Creek Old House—the former residence of Liu Wenqi, one of the most important representatives of the Yangzhou School in the Qing Dynasty. Undoubtedly, the most famous of the residences is the Wangs' Residence, which is under protection of Jiangsu Province.

The Wangs' Residence

The Wangs' Residence is one of the best preserved residences of the salt merchants in the late Qing Dynasty and the early Republic of China.

In the Wangs' Residence, there are three lines of houses, each consisting of three rows. The houses are arranged on the same north-south axis, and the wing rooms on both sides are symmetrical bilaterally, which reflects the Golden Mean of Confucianism. The residence with a balanced and inter-connected layout, benefits from good ventilation and daylight. Each part can stand on its own, but can also be a part of the whole structure. The Wangs' Residence, a typical ancient residence, best exemplifies the traditional architectural style of the grand mansions in Yangzhou. In front of and behind the houses are three exquisite gardens, namely the Keqi Garden (meaning "garden suitable for residence"), the Xiaoyuanchunshen Garden (meaning "small garden in mid-spring") and the Yingxi Garden (meaning "garden of welcoming the morning sun"). The gardens incorporated into the residence enhance the pleasant and ever-changing atmosphere of the private garden-like residence.

The exquisite wood, brick, and stone carvings together with their precious materials, diverse techniques, rich themes and profound cultural connotations are combined skillfully with the walls and floors, to complement to each other's beauty.

The Historic District of Renfengli

East of the Wenhe Road and west of the Guoqing Road, Renfengli, a historic street, runs from south to north. The district ranges from the Small Qinhuai River in the east, the Caoli Lane in the south, the Yingchun Lane and the Shi Lane in the west, and the Seven Lane in the north.

In this district, No.6 to No.8 on the Yuxian Street are the Former Residence of Ruan Yuan, a key figure of Yangzhou School and a senior provincial official in the Qing Dynasty. Next to it, on the southeast corner, is the Jingzhong Temple, a famous temple in the old Yangzhou city.

阮元故居

阮元曾被清代道光皇帝誉为“极三朝之恩遇，为一代之完人”，其故居建于1804年，现为省级文物保护单位。过去门前有牌坊，上书“文官下轿，武官下马”。整个建筑群分东、中、西三路。东、西两路为宅第，中路为家庙。

· 阮氏家庙

东路第一、二进分别为门厅、大厅，是近两年复建的，后面三进为原物，一直为阮元后人居住，保存得相当完好；天井开阔，建筑考究，庄重气派，古韵犹存。西路只有后进三间两厢的平房为原物，其余都为近两年复建。

中路为阮氏家庙，临街院墙中间嵌石刻横额“太傅文达阮公家庙”八个大字，至今完好。大门厅、二门厅、庙堂等原有建筑尚存。

目前正拟将阮元故居建设成为扬州学派纪念馆，以对外开放。

匏庐

匏（匏读piáo）庐位于甘泉路，紧挨在仁丰里街区南边，为民国初年淮扬道尹卢殿虎所建。该园以横长别致著称，小中见大，别有洞天，由狭巷进入，分左右两小院，形如瓢葫芦，故称“匏庐”。

匏庐保存尚好，为省级文物保护单位，现刚翻建，不久将对外开放。

The Former Residence of Ruan Yuan

Ruan Yuan was praised by Emperor Daoguang in the Qing Dynasty as "a scholar-official appreciated by three succeeding emperors, a perfect person of his generation". His residence was built in 1804 and is now a cultural heritage under protection of Jiangsu Province. There used to be a monumental gateway with the inscription "Civilian alighting; Military attache dismounting". The whole complex is divided into the east, the middle and the west parts. The east and west parts are for residence, while the middle part is the ancestral temple.

The eastern building complex consists of five rows of houses. The first and second houses are respectively the foyer and the grand hall, which have been restored to their original state in recent two years. The other three houses in the back are the original ones and are remarkably preserved. Ruan Yuan's descendants have been living here. The grand residential area with spacious courtyards is built in an elegant architectural style with old features, which creates a solemn atmosphere. As for the west part, the only original building is the back house with three main rooms and two wing-rooms. The rest of the west building complex has been restored to their original state in the recent years.

The middle part is the ancestral temple, in whose courtyard wall adjacent to the street is carved a stone banner with eight Chinese characters "太傅文达阮公家庙". The Gate Hall, the Second Hall and the ancestral temple are well preserved in their original condition.

The Former Residence of Ruan Yuan is to be open to the public as the Memorial Hall of Yangzhou School.

Piao Lu

Located in the Ganquan Road, close to the southern part of the Renfengli area, Piao Lu was built by Lu Dianhu, the prefect of Huaiyang in the early Republic of China. The long and narrow garden is known for its uniqueness. A narrow lane will lead visitors right to the garden with two small yards, one on the left and the other on the right. Piao Lu owes its name to the fact that it has the shape of a gourd. Here, the visitors can fully appreciate the art of expanding the small space of a garden to the infinite.

As a cultural relic under protection of Jiangsu Province, Piao Lu is in good condition. It has just been reconstructed and will soon be open to the public.

湾子街历史文化街区

该街区东至皮市街附近，西至永胜街，南至广陵路，北至古旗亭街、玉井巷一线，重点保护该区朴实的民俗风情以及独特的街巷格局。

街区内作为市级文物加以保护的有古井三口、名人故居两处、盐商住宅两处、园林宅第一处、传统民居三处。其中三多巷10号就是当年闻名全国的评话大师、中国曲艺工作者协会副主席王少堂的故居。

朱自清故居

琼花观对面窄长的巷子是安乐巷，现代著名散文家、诗人朱自清的故居就座落在该巷中。这座老宅建于清代，是典型的扬州传统民居。房屋保护良好，环境静雅，已被列为国家级文物保护单位。故居第一进里陈列着朱自清当年用的家具和他的部分手稿；第二进为他生平事迹展，分序厅和展厅，西厢房的序厅中央伫立着朱自清先生的塑像。

· 朱自清故居

吴道台宅第

吴道台宅第在扬州市第一人民医院南侧。吴道台名叫吴引孙，在光绪年间任浙江宁绍台道道员。他聘请浙江工匠来扬营建私宅。整个建筑群呈方形，边长100米，规模宏大，结构精巧，雕工精致，以浙江建造法为基础，又揉合了扬州传统的建筑工艺，为扬州古建筑中独具一格的住宅建筑群。宅第内的“测海楼”，是二十世纪初闻名大江南北的藏书楼。上个世纪，从这个宅第中先后走出了好几位享誉全国的学者。

· 吴道台宅第外观

The Historical District of the Wanzi Street

This historical area stretches from the Pishi Street in the east to the Yongsheng Street in the west, from the Guangling Road in the south to the Guqi Pavilion Street and the Yujing Lane in the north. The efforts focus on preserving the folk customs and the unique pattern of streets and alleys.

In this area, three wells, two former residences of celebrities, two former residences of salt merchants, one garden and three traditional houses are protected as municipal heritage. The mansion at No.10 the Sanduo Lane, is the former residence of Wang Shaotang, the famous master of storytelling and the vice president of the Chinese Folk Art Association.

The Former Residence of Zhu Ziqing

The Former Residence of Zhu Ziqing, a well-known modern essayist and poet, is located in the Anle Lane, opposite the Qionghua Taoist Temple. Built in the Qing Dynasty, the house is a typical traditional dwelling in Yangzhou. The environment here is quiet and pleasant. It is in good condition and has been listed as a historical and cultural heritage under the national-level protection. The furniture used by Zhu Ziqing and some of his manuscripts are exhibited here. Zhu Ziqing's life stories are on display in the back of the building complex, which is divided into the introduction hall and the exhibition hall. In the west wing room stands a statue of Mr. Zhu Ziqing.

The Wu Daotai's Mansion

The Wu Daotai's Mansion is located to the south of Yangzhou No.1 People's Hospital. Wu Yinsun, the owner of the residence, was once the head of the Ningbo-Shaoxing region in Zhejiang Province during the reign of Emperor Guangxu in the Qing Dynasty. The mansion is a Zhejiang-style complex, because he had his construction ideas carried out by the craftsmen from Zhejiang. The complex is in the shape of a square, measuring 100 meters on each side. The architecture is mostly of Zhejiang style, at the same time featuring traditional Yangzhou characteristics. It boasts a grand scale, delicate structure and exquisite carving techniques, giving it a class of its own. The Cehai Pagoda in the complex was renowned in the beginning of the 20th century for its rich book collection. No wonder that this mansion with a strong literary spirit was the birthplace of and home to several scholars with national fame in the 20th century.

南河下历史文化街区

本街区东至徐凝门路，南至南河下街，西至傅家甸、达士巷一线，北至广陵路。该街区历史上曾是盐商居住和贸易的主要场所，街区内目前保留着诸多盐商住宅及会馆，建筑高大精美，在数量、规模上都列在各街区之首。名宅比较集中的古街是南河下街、新仓巷和丁家湾。

卢绍绪宅第

· 卢绍绪宅第

卢绍绪宅第位于康山街22号，是扬州晚清盐商住宅中数一数二的豪宅。此宅建于清光绪年间，当年兴建此宅历时三年多，耗银七万余两。卢宅曾前后进深达190米，占地一万余平方米。从外表看，古宅青砖黛瓦，与一般住宅无异，但置身其中，淮海厅、兰馨厅、涵碧厅、怡情楼，厅厅相连，厅堂阔大，可设宴百席，气派非凡。

卢氏古宅现已成为品味淮扬饮食文化与清代盐商建筑文化的清雅之处。

The Historical and Cultural Block of Nanhexia

The block of Nanhexia (South canalside) borders the Xuningmen Road in the east, the Nanhexia Street in the south, the Fujiadian and the Dashi Lane in the west, and the Guangling Road in the north. This block used to be the residential and commercial area for the salt merchants and officials. Even today this neighborhood is mostly well-known for the large number of mansions of salt merchants and assembly halls with grand and exquisite architectural style. Those famous mansions are especially concentrated in the Nanhexia Street, the Xincang Lane and the Dingjia Bay.

The Lu Shaoxu's Mansion

Built during the reign of Emperor Guangxu, the Lu Shaoxu's Mansion at No. 22 the Kang Shan Street is known as one of the most luxurious houses of salt merchants in the late Qing Dynasty in Yangzhou. Reportedly, it took Lu Shaoxu over seventy thousand taels of siver and three years to build this mansion. It used to cover an area of ten thousand square meters, the distance from front to back reaching 190 meters. From the outside, the grey bricks and tiles look no different in size and shape from those of ordinary houses. However, once inside, tourists will be amazed at the largest complex of interconnected halls in Yangzhou, among which are the Huaihai Hall, the Lanxin Hall, the Hanbi Hall and the Yiqing Building. The halls are said to be spacious enough to accomodate 100 tables for a banquet.

The Lu Shaoxu's Mansion has now become a fabulous place to savor the Huaiyang cuisine and the architectural style of the salt merchants' residence of Yangzhou in the Qing Dynasty.

第四节　古刹名寺

扬州古刹名寺众多。天宁寺、大明寺、观音寺、石塔寺、旌忠寺等寺庙历史悠久，都是始建于东晋或南北朝时期。

大明寺

大明寺位于扬州城西北蜀冈中峰上，始建于南朝刘宋大明年间。隋代，皇帝下令在此建造雄伟的栖灵塔。唐代，大明寺住持鉴真东渡日本弘扬佛法。宋代，欧阳修在此修筑平山堂。清代，康熙、乾隆二帝曾多次巡游平山堂和大明寺，作诗题字，极盛一时。

· 大明寺

大明寺集佛教寺庙、人文胜迹和园林风光于一体，一千多年来，更享有“淮东第一胜境”之美名。

大明寺景区的游览主体可以分为三个部分，即大明寺、鉴真纪念堂、平山堂。

沿着康熙、乾隆御道拾级而上，迎面见到的是“栖灵遗址”牌坊。穿过山门殿，殿的北侧两株茂盛的银杏树高大挺拔。再往北，便是三重檐歇山顶的大雄宝殿了。

寺院东部是巍峨的栖灵塔。唐代许多大诗人如李白、高适、白居易、刘禹锡等都曾登临此塔，并赋诗赞咏。

· 栖灵塔玉佛

Section Four Ancient Temples

There are many renowned ancient temples and monasteries in Yangzhou, such as the Tianning Temple, the Daming Temple, the Guanyin Temple, the Stone Pagoda and the Jingzhong Temple. All these temples were all first constructed either in the Eastern Jin Dynasty or the Southern and Northern Dynasties.

The Daming Temple

Initially built during the Daming Period of Liu Song Dynasty in the Southern Dynasty, the Daming Temple is located on the hillside of the Shugang Ridge in the northwestern suburb of Yangzhou. In the Sui Dynasty, the emperor had the magnificent Qiling Tower erected at the site. In the Tang Dynasty, the abbot of the Daming Temple Jian Zhen ferried across to Japan to preach Buddhism. The Pingshan Hall was built here in the Northern Song Dynasty when the famous man of letters Ou Yangxiu was the mayor of Yangzhou. The Daming Temple enjoyed its peak fame in the Qing Dynasty when Emperors Qianlong and Kangxi visited Yangzhou several times, touring the Pingshan Hall and the Daming Temple, writing many verses and leaving their calligraphy works here.

The Daming Temple, known as No. 1 Temple East of the Huai River for 1,000 years, is famous for its perfect integration of the classic gardens, cultural and historic relics, and Buddhism architectural features.

The Daming Temple Scenic Spot mainly consists of three parts, the temple complex, the Memorial Hall of Master Jian Zhen and the Pingshan Hall.

Following the Kangxi-Qianlong Royal Road, you will be greeted by an ancient decorated archway bearing the inscription of "Ruins of Qiling". After going through the Gate Hall, you will find two ancient ginkgo trees growing lavishly to the north of the hall. Further north stands the main hall of the temple, called the Treasure Hall of the Great Sage, or the Mahavira Hall, which is a one story structure with a triple-eave hipped roof.

To the east of the Daming Temple stands the high Qiling Tower. In the Tang Dynasty many a great poet and literati like Li Bai, Gao Shi, Bai Juyi and Liu Yuxi visited and climbed the glorious tower and wrote inspiring verses. The present Qiling Tower, a nine-story structure with

现在的栖灵塔于1995年复建竣工，为唐代风格，九层四面，高70米。塔周围的钟楼、鼓楼、卧佛殿等呈拱卫状。塔的第一层供奉着四尊面目清秀、仪态庄重的玉佛，他们是1996年缅甸仰光市市长吴歌礼赠送的。塔的第二层供奉着2003年日本唐招提寺赠送给大明寺的三颗佛祖舍利子，他们是当年由鉴真带去日本的。

鉴真纪念堂主体建筑紧挨在大雄宝殿的东北边，是一组仿唐式四合院，完全仿照日本唐招提寺的金堂建造，只是缩小了些。纪念堂碑亭内的纪念碑是一座卧式碑，正面的“唐鉴真大和尚纪念碑”为郭沫若所题。纪念堂中央供奉的是鉴真大师的干漆夹纻坐像。

· 鉴真纪念堂

鉴真纪念堂主体建筑的南面为鉴真东渡史料陈列室，是一座清式四合院。

鉴真是扬州人，也是当时著名的高僧，长期住持大明寺。他的东渡，对日本的佛教、文学、建筑、雕塑、医药、书法、印刷、手工生产等方面产生了深远的影响。因此，鉴真被奉为“日本律宗祖师”、“医药之祖”、“文化恩人”。

平山堂位于大雄宝殿的西面，是欧阳修建造的一处休闲厅堂。欧阳修是北宋著名政治家，他在中央全力支持范仲淹的政治改革。改革失败后，他被贬为地方官，曾任扬州太守。欧阳修为人豁达豪放，被贬后常寄情于山水诗酒。

· 平山堂

平山堂高踞蜀岗之上，视野极为开阔，其雄伟、儒雅，在江淮地区可谓首屈一指。每当有来自远方的文人雅士拜访，欧阳修在处理完繁忙的公务之后，就会带着客人们来此凭栏览胜，对酒赏月，传花赋诗。

多年以后，欧阳修的学生苏东坡也来到扬州任太守。他在平山堂后面

four facades reaching 70 meters in height, was reconstructed in 1995 in the style of the Tang Dynasty. Clustered around the tower are the Bell Tower, the Drum Tower, and the Reclining Buddha Temple. On the first floor of the tower are four magnificent and solemn jade Buddhas, given as a gift from Mayor Wu Geli of Yangon, Myanmar. On the second floor, there are three pieces of Sakyamuni Buddha relics enshrined, which were taken to Japan by Jian Zhen and returned in 2003 by Japan's Toshodai-ji.

The main building of the Memorial Hall of Master Jian Zhen is located to the northeast of the Mahavira Hall. The design adhered to the norms of the quadrangle courtyard of the Tang Dynasty and at the same time borrowed the architectural feature of the Classic Golden Hall of Japan's Toshodai-ji. The monument inside bears a horizontal inscription by Guo Moruo "The Monument to Master Jian Zhen of the Tang Dynasty". A gauze-and-lacquer statue of Jian Zhen in a sitting position is placed in the center of the main hall of this memorial. South of the main hall is the showroom of Jian Zhen's sailing to Japan, a square courtyard in Qing style.

Jian Zhen, a famous master of Buddhism in the Tang Dynasty, was a Yangzhou native. He resided in the Daming Temple as the abbot for many years before his departure to Japan. Jian Zhen's sailing to Japan exerted great influences on Japanese Buddhist culture, literature, architecture, sculpture, medicine, calligraphy, printing and handicraft industries. For his great contribution to Japan, Jian Zhen was worshipped by Japanese people as the Founder of Japanese Vinaya School, Ancestor of Japanese Medicine, and Benefactor of Japanese Culture.

To the west of the Mahavira Hall is the Pingshan Hall, a hall for leisure and entertainment, which was constructed by Ou Yangxiu. As a famous statesman and a man of letters in the Northern Song Dynasty, Ou Yangxiu, with a bold character and an open mind, whole-heartedly supported Fan Zhongyan's political reform. After the failure of the reform, he was demoted to a local magistrate, the prefect of Yangzhou, where he found solace in poetry, wine and beautiful landscape.

Perched high on the Shugang Ridge, the Pingshan Hall enjoys a panoramic view. Its magnificence and elegance is second to none in the Jianghuai region. In their free time, Ou Yangxiu and his friends of literary circles often held parties here to enjoy the beautiful scenery and write poems while quaffing the wine.

Years later, Su Dongpo, Ou Yangxiu's student, took office as prefect in Yangzhou. In memory of his mentor, he built the Gulin Hall behind

建了谷林堂，以纪念他的老师。康熙、乾隆二帝对欧阳修的为人、为政、为文向来敬佩，每次南巡到扬州，总要来此缅怀一番。

天宁寺

天宁寺位于盐阜路北侧。清代，天宁寺位居当时扬州八大名刹之首。清代两帝南巡时，康熙有两次到达天宁寺行宫，而乾隆则有五次。行宫旁有御花园，寺前砌了御马头，祖孙二帝多次由御马头坐龙舟去平山堂观光赏景。两位皇帝先后赐给天宁寺匾额十一块，楹联十幅，并赋诗若干赞美该寺。曹雪芹的祖父曹寅曾奉皇命在天宁寺组织刊刻《全唐诗》和《佩文韵府》。乾隆时编写的中国最大的一部丛书《四库全书》，其中一套就藏于天宁寺行宫内的文汇阁。

·天宁寺山门

目前天宁寺是一组房屋多达92间的巍峨建筑群，气势雄伟，布局严整，但这仅仅是她过去的一小部分。多年前，天宁寺曾作过扬州博物馆。现在，仍有不少文物保存在这里。

高旻寺

在扬子江南路西侧的三汊河岸边，有一处巍峨壮丽的宝刹，这就是被誉为清代禅宗四大寺院之一的高旻寺。

康熙帝第四次南巡时，曾登临寺中的天中塔，并赐寺名“高旻寺”。之后曹寅在寺西建成规模宏大的塔湾行宫。康熙帝后来的两次南巡，以及乾隆帝的所有六次南巡，都曾住在塔湾行宫。

·高旻寺

the Pingshan Hall. Besides, Emperors Kangxi and Qianlong admired Ou Yangxiu for his personality, statesmanship and essays so much that they came here to reminisce him each time they went on their southern inspection tours.

The Tianning Temple

Located on the north side of the Yanfu Road, the Tianning Temple ranked first among the eight famous temples in Yangzhou in the Qing Dynasty. Emperors Kangxi and Qianlong went on six inspection tours to southern China. Emperor Kangxi visited and stayed in the Tianning temple, one of his royal residences in Yangzhou, twice, while Emperor Qianlong camped here five times. Beside the royal residence was a royal garden. In front of the temple, there stood a royal dock, from which Emperors Kangxi and Qianlong, took the dragon boats to the Pingshan Hall to enjoy the scenery respectively. The two emperors presented the Tianning Temple eleven horizontally-inscribed boards, ten couplets and many poems that they wrote in praise of the temple. The Tianning Temple was associated with, Cao Yin, Cao Xueqin's grandfather, who organized the editing and publication of *The Complete Poetry of the Tang Dynasty* and *Payvand Rhyme* at the order of the emperor. Emperor Qianlong himself sponsored the compilation of Si Ku Quan Shu (*Complete Library of the Four Branches of Literature*), one copy was kept in the Wenhui Pavilion in the Tianning royal residence.

The majestic temple, exquisitely laid out, is a building complex containing up to 92 rooms. However, the present-day temple is only a fraction of what it used to be. Many years ago, it was used as Yangzhou Museum. Nowadays, a large number of historical artifacts and cultural relics are still kept here.

The Gaomin Temple

On the Sancha River bank, west of the Yangtze River South Road, there stands the majestic Gaomin Temple, known as one of the four greatest Zen monasteries in the Qing Dynasty.

On his fourth southern tour, Emperor Kangxi climbed the Tianzhong Tower in this temple and named the temple Gaomin Temple. Later, to the west of the temple, Cao Yin built Tawan royal residence—grand-scale lodging for the emperors when they carried out their inspections of Yangzhou. Both Emperors Kangxi and Qianlong stayed at the residence, twice and six times respectively, on their southern tours.

现今高旻寺山门上嵌有康熙帝手书的“敕建高旻寺”汉白玉石额，寺内许多建筑已相继完成重建工作。寺内曾有一座金佛殿，里面供奉着康熙帝赠予的金佛。御碑亭内镌刻着康熙帝作的《高旻寺碑记》。三百年来，高旻寺衣钵相传，高僧辈出，直至今日。该寺不仅享誉国内，也受到东南亚国家佛教界的敬仰。寺内现有缅甸寺院赠送的立、卧玉佛各一尊，为古刹增添了不少光辉。

仙鹤寺

仙鹤寺在扬州老城区南门街上，为江苏省文物保护单位。它与广州怀圣寺（也称狮子寺）、泉州清净寺（也称麒麟寺）、杭州凤凰寺并称我国东南沿海地区伊斯兰教四大名寺。

·仙鹤寺

仙鹤寺坐西朝东，建于南宋末年，据传是由伊斯兰教创始人穆罕默德的第十六世孙普哈丁募资建造的。礼拜殿南边的银杏树，是南宋时栽植的。仙鹤寺保留了不少明代建筑的遗物，目前是扬州市区穆斯林的主要活动场所，扬州市伊斯兰教协会也在此办公。

扬州天主堂和扬州基督堂

扬州天主堂也称耶稣圣心堂，位于市区跃进桥西侧北河下25号，始建于1864年。教堂坐西朝东，占地面积2080平方米，建筑面积1302平方米。教堂为中世纪哥特式建筑，屋尖竖铜十字架，正面有三拱门，两侧有钟楼。窗户镶嵌彩色玻璃，装修精致华美。教

·扬州天主堂

Above the main gate of the Gaomin Temple is a white marble lintel engraved with Emperor Kangxi's handwriting "The Gaomin Temple Built under Imperial Order". Inside the temple many buildings have been successively reconstructed. In the temple there is a Gold Buddha Hall, dedicated to a gold Buddha presented by Emperor Kangxi. Further, you will find two Imperial Stele Pavilions facing each other, in which the steles are engraved with "Epigraph on the Gaomin Temple", written by Emperor Kangxi. In the past 300 years, large numbers of respected monks in the Gaomin Temple have been passing down the legacy of Buddhism from generation to generation. The temple is not only well known at home, but also worshiped by Buddhists from Southeast Asia. Besides, the Standing Buddha and the Reclining Jade Buddha from Myanmar add brilliance to the temple.

The Fairy Crane Mosque

Located in the South Gate Street in the old city of Yangzhou, the Fairy Crane Mosque is on the list of cultural heritages under protection of Jiangsu Province. Along with the Huaisheng Mosque in Guangzhou (also known as the Lion Mosque), the Qingjing Mosque in Quanzhou (also known as the Kirin Mosque) and the Phoenix Mosque in Hangzhou, they are regarded as four major mosques in the southeast of China.

Built in the late Southern Song Dynasty, the Fairy Crane Mosque sits west and faces east. Legend has it that Puhaddin, the 16th generation descendant of Mohamed, raised the funds to build the mosque. The ginkgo tree to the south of the Worship Hall was planted in the Southern Song Dynasty. Fortunately, there survived many architectural relics of the Ming Dynasty in the mosque. At present, the Fairy Crane Mosque is the main venue for Muslim activities as well as the workplace for Yangzhou Islamic Association.

Yangzhou Catholic Church and Yangzhou Church of Christ

Known as the Hall of Sacred Heart of Jesus and built in 1864, Yangzhou Catholic Church is located at No. 25 the Beihexia Street on the west side of the Yuejin Bridge. Sitting west and facing east, the church covers an area of 2,080 square meters with the construction area of 1,302 square meters. The church is built in medieval Gothic architectural style, with a vertical copper cross on the roof, three front arches and a bell tower on each side. Its windows are decorated with colored glass mosaic, beautiful and exquisite. On the south side is a well preserved Priest

堂南边有神父楼一座，保存完好。教堂现在常举行宗教活动，也是省级文物保护单位。

扬州基督堂在萃园路2号，紧靠国庆路，始建于1923年，1985年修整一新。教堂座北朝南，十字脊屋顶，鱼鳞瓦屋面，平面布局仿美国近百年来的教堂形式，使用面积1020平方米。中间大厅内不用一根柱子，可供400人同时做礼拜用，气势旷达。拉开两侧与各教室间的隔板，大厅则可容纳1000人。

Building. Religious activities are often held in the church, which is also a cultural heritage under protection of Jiangsu Province.

Yangzhou Church of Christ is located at No. 2 the Cuiyuan Road, next to the Guoqing Road. First built in 1923 and repaired in 1985, the church, with a cross ridged roof tiled in fish-scale patterns, sits north and faces south. The layout is a copy of American church style of the last one hundred years. It occupies a usable floor area of 1,020 square meters. There is no pillar in the middle of the hall, but it is spacious enough for 400 worshipers at a time. If the clapboards on both sides of the hall are taken away, it can hold up to 1,000 people at a time.

第五节　古墓名祠

在扬州附近的丘陵地区，有不少古墓葬，其中大多数是汉代的，包括汉代诸藩王的大型墓葬。扬州古墓葬中，文物价值最高的当数汉广陵王墓。而隋炀帝杨广的陵墓也在扬州近郊。董子祠和史公祠是扬州市两处著名的名人祠堂。

董子祠

董子祠位于老城区北柳巷99号，是祭祀汉代儒家学派著名人物董仲舒的祠堂。董子祠建于明朝初年，大殿雄伟，用料讲究，是扬州现存的为数不多的明代建筑之一。

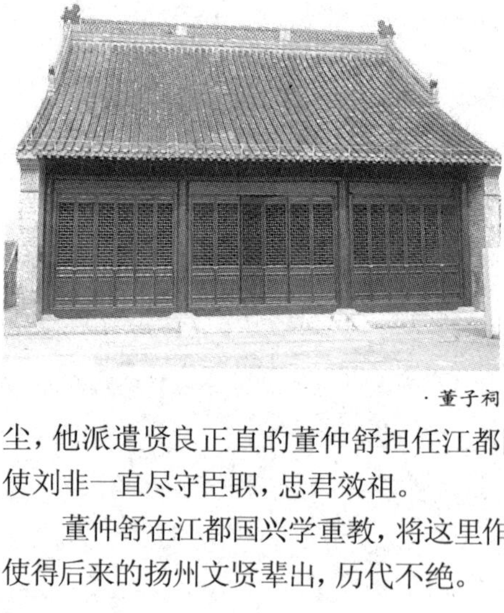

· 董子祠

董仲舒是汉代著名的思想家、哲学家、教育家，他的“罢黜百家，独尊儒术”的主张被汉武帝采纳。从此，儒家学说成为官方正统哲学思想，并延续了两千年。

“七国之乱”后，汉景帝改吴国为江都国，封儿子刘非为江都王。汉武帝知道哥哥刘非骄奢好胜，为防止刘非步刘濞后尘，他派遣贤良正直的董仲舒担任江都国相，对刘非加以辅佐匡正，果然使刘非一直尽守臣职，忠君效祖。

董仲舒在江都国兴学重教，将这里作为其儒学思想的实行、推广基地，使得后来的扬州文贤辈出，历代不绝。

汉陵苑

汉陵苑又称汉广陵王墓博物馆，位于平山堂东路北侧，坐落在保障湖

Section Five Ancient Tombs and Temples

In the hilly areas around Yangzhou, there are many ancient tombs, most of which date back to the Han Dynasty, including the large burial sites of kings. Among them, the tomb of King Guangling in the Han Dynasty values the highest. The Mausoleum of Emperor Yang in the Sui Dynasty lies in the suburbs of Yangzhou. In Yangzhou, you will also find the ancestral temples dedicated to two historical figures, namely, the Dongzi Ancestral Temple and the Shi Kefa Memorial Hall.

The Dongzi Ancestral Temple

The Dongzi (Dong Zhongshu) Ancestral Temple is located at No. 99 the Beiliu Lane in the old city. It is a place to worship the great Confucianism scholar in the Han Dynasty. With its majestic hall and selected building materials, the Dongzi Ancestral Temple is one of the few buildings survived from the Ming Dynasty.

Dong Zhongshu was a famous thinker, philosopher and educator of the Han Dynasty. His idea of "proscribing all non-Confucian schools of thought and espousing Confucianism as the orthodox state ideology" was adopted by Emperor Wu of the Han Dynasty. For two thousand years thereafter, Confucianism was the only dominant school of thought in China.

After the Rebellion of the Seven States, Emperor Jing of the Han Dynasty had the State of Wu renamed as Jiangdu, and made his son Liu Fei the King of Jiangdu. Emperor Wu of the Han Dynasty, Emperor Jing's tenth child and his successor, knew his brother Liu Fei was somewhat arrogant, conceited and combative. Therefore, to prevent Liu Fei from becoming another Liu Bi, he appointed Dong Zhongshu as prime minister of Jiangdu Kingdom to assist Liu Fei. Just as Emperor Wu of the Han Dynasty had hoped, Liu Fei remained capable of performing his duties, faithful to the emperor and devoted to the state.

Dong Zhongshu set up schools and advocated education in the Kingdom of Jiangdu, making it the base to promote and practice Confucianism. Since then, each generation never failed to produce many literati.

The Han Mausoleum

The Han Mausoleum, also called the Mausoleum Museum of

东北边的蜀岗上。这是一座古朴雄浑的园林式主题博物馆，建筑风格仿照汉代。

汉武帝的哥哥刘非去世后，刘非的儿子刘建继位为江都王。从小养尊处优的刘建，后来联络淮南王刘安等人，企图谋反，最终自缢身亡。刘建的女儿刘细君后来远嫁乌孙国，成为"汉家和亲第一公主"。刘建自杀后，汉武帝改江都国为广陵国，册封自己的儿子刘胥为广陵王。

扬州城西北40多公里处有一石山名为神居山，也称天山。1979年春，考古工作者发掘出两座大型西汉墓葬，两墓是帝王级的"黄肠题凑"木椁墓。经考证，墓主是西汉广陵王刘胥及其王后。该墓在全国已出土的十座同类型墓葬中，规模最大，结构最复杂，用料最考究，保存最完整。为更好地保护墓葬，后将这两墓迁至扬州，用原墓构件、按原墓式样重建，并建立了汉广陵王墓博物馆。

· 汉广陵王刘胥棺椁

汉广陵王墓博物馆的展区主要有四部分：一是"广陵潮涌"陈列室，介绍汉代时期的扬州历史；二是"广陵王地宫"，展出刘胥的黄肠题凑木椁墓；三是"王后寝宫"，展出王后的黄肠题凑木椁墓；四是"细君出塞"，介绍江都公主刘细君为和亲远嫁乌孙的事迹。

King Guangling in the Han Dynasty, is located on the Shugang Ridge northeast of the Baozhang Lake, north of the Pingshan Hall East Road. This garden-style museum is modeled after the old and simple architectural style of the Han Dynasty.

After Liu Fei died, his son Liu Jian, who was born into a privileged background and brought up in luxury, succeeded to the throne as the King of Jiangdu. Liu Jian joined the King of Huainan, Liu An, in attempting a rebellion against the Han throne, but failed and ultimately hanged himself. Later, Liu Jian's daughter, Liu Xijun, also known as the Princess of Jiangdu, was married to the King of Wusun State and became "the first diplomatic bride in Chinese history". After Liu Jian committed suicide, Emperor Wu of the Han Dynasty renamed Jiangdu as Guangling and appointed his son Liu Xu as the King of Guangling.

More than 40 kilometers northwest of Yangzhou city stands the Shenju Mountain, also known as the Heaven Mountain. In the spring of 1979, archaeologists discovered two large Western Han tombs. Research shows that the two Huang Chang Ti Cou tombs (a unique burial practice in the Han Dynasty, with cypress wood encasing the coffin) were built for Liu Xu, the first-generation Guangling King in the Mid-Western Han Dynasty, and his queen. The coffins are both equally encased in a cypress frame, which was the customary burial practice of emperors in the Han Dynasty. The mausoleum boasts a magnificent scale and complex structure and is well preserved, which is a rare case among the ten similar tombs unearthed throughout the country. For the sake of better protecting the mausoleum, the two tombs were moved from their original site to Yangzhou city, properly reconstructed with the original tomb components in their original positions. Thus, the Mausoleum Museum of King Guangling in the Han Dynasty was re-established.

The exhibition area of the museum is mainly divided into four parts. Section one is the showroom for Guangling Tide, which focuses on the history of Yangzhou in the Han Dynasty. Section two is called Underground Palace for the King of Guangling, featuring Liu Xu's imperial wooden coffin of Huang Chang Ti Cou style. Section three is for The Queen's Palace, displaying the queen's tomb of the same style. The Fourth section Xijun Crossing the Frontier presents the moving deeds of Liu Xijun, the Princess of Jiangdu. In order to safeguard the peace of the state, she voluntarily married the King of Wusun State and lived far away from her motherland.

经复原，刘胥棺木四周的木椁，南北长近17米，东西宽14米多，通高4.5米，由857块楠木构件拼接而成，其中有相当的部分是金丝楠木。王后墓的木椁稍小。两座墓的棺椁共使用楠木1000立方米，不用一根钉子，堪称鬼斧神工。

广陵王墓出土了近千件文物，对研究汉代人的生活极有价值。墓中还出土了大量文字资料，为研究汉代的文化艺术提供了宝贵的实物参考。

隋炀帝陵

扬州城北槐泗镇雷塘北侧，坐落着隋炀帝杨广的陵墓。杨广曾在广陵做过十年的扬州总管，对扬州颇有感情，喜欢说南方话。

· 隋炀帝杨广像

隋炀帝相貌堂堂，武艺很好，喜爱读书著述，诗也写得很不错。隋炀帝第一次下扬州，在扬州呆了八个月。第二次下扬州，在扬州呆了近一年。隋炀帝好大喜功，特别喜欢讲排场，在扬州建了很多行宫。第三次下扬州时，他日日沉湎酒色，无意北归。他的奢侈、荒淫、暴虐，给人民带来了巨大的苦难，终于引得天下大乱。公元618年，起义军逼近，杨广被其部下勒死于扬州行宫，隋朝灭亡。

“入郭登桥出郭船，红楼日日柳年年。君王忍把平陈业，只换雷塘数亩田。”隋炀帝的一生，留给我们后人的是无尽的感慨。

After the restoration, Liu Xu's coffin complex is discovered to be nearly 17 meters long from north to south, 14 meters wide from east to west and 4.5 meters high. It is composed of 857 blocks of Nanmu, a considerable part of them being the golden Nanmu. The coffin of the queen was slightly smaller. The two burial chambers were built of a total of 1,000 cubic meters of Nanmu without using a single nail, which was considered a wonder.

In all, nearly 1,000 pieces of cultural relics were unearthed in the Mausoleum of the Han Dynasty. These artifacts are extremely valuable for the study of daily life in the Han Dynasty. Besides, a large number of unearthed written historical materials also provide priceless reference for researching the culture and arts of the Han Dynasty.

The Mausoleum of Emperor Yang in the Sui Dynasty

North of Lei Tang (Thunder Pool), the Huaisi Town in the northern suburbs of Yangzhou lies Emperor Yang's mausoleum. Emperor Yang, personal name Yang Guang, had been the governor of Guangling for 10 years before he was crowned prince. He fell in love with Yangzhou at the first sight and he preferred to speak the southern dialect.

Emperor Yang was considered handsome and intelligent in his youth, and was skilled in poetry, martial arts and even authored some books. On his first tour to Yangzhou, he lingered here for eight months. And the second time he came to Yangzhou, he stayed for nearly a year. Emperor Yang especially enjoyed an extravagant lifestyle and built many royal residences in Yangzhou. The third time, he overindulged himself in wine and lust, without intending to go back to the capital to handle state affairs. His abundant expense, tyranny and prurience caused people much suffering and left the empire die out and the country in turbulence. As a result, peasant uprisings broke out one after another. In 618, Emperor Yang was strangled by his followers in one of his palaces in Yangzhou, and the Sui Dynasty ended.

"Emperor Yang made three voyages on a most luxurious imperial ship to Jiangdu (present-day Yangzhou), where day after day, year after year, he indulged himself in pleasure; how could he trade the vast territory conquered and unified by his father, Emperor Wen of the Sui Dynasty, for several acres of his graveyard in Lei Tang after he was eventually killed?" This poem illustrates that Emperor Yang's prurience and immoderate expenses led to the doom of the Sui Dynasty, which leaves us so much for reflection and pondering.

史公祠

史公祠今称史可法纪念馆，位于天宁寺东侧梅花岭，为全国重点文物保护单位，也是一处融历史、文物、风景于一体的游览胜地。

1645年春，身为东阁大学士兼兵部尚书的史可法督师江淮，守卫扬州。清豫亲王多铎多次派人送信劝降，但史可法在外援断绝、军饷不继的情况下，不为所动，以忠义激励军民继续坚守孤城，誓与扬州城共存亡。扬州城失陷后，史可法自杀未遂被俘。多铎劝其投降，并许以高官，史可法大义凛然，严词拒绝，遂被杀害，时年44岁。清军在扬州屠城十天，史称“扬州十日”。之后，史可法的义子史德威遍寻遗骸不得，只好将史公生前遗物葬于城北梅花岭下。

飨堂是史公祠的主体建筑。飨堂前有一副非常有名的楹联：“数点梅花亡国泪，二分明月故臣心。”飨堂中央端坐着史公的塑像，后面便是史公之墓。

梅花岭后有一建筑“晴雪轩”，轩中陈列的是史可法的遗墨，所以又称“遗墨厅”。遗墨厅内，有史公《复多尔衮书》、《临难家书》和其他墨迹联对。

史公祠堂在飨堂的西边，祠中有史可法的画像、神龛、牌位，以及同时殉难的其他官员的牌位。乾隆皇帝“褒慰忠魂”题词的石刻拓片也在祠内。

· 飨堂

The Shi Kefa Memorial Hall

On the Plum Blossom Hill, east of the Tianning Temple, stands the Shi Kefa Memorial Hall, a temple devoted to the hero Shi Kefa. It's an important cultural heritage under the national-level protection, as well as a major tourist attraction with history, culture and scenery perfectly blended together.

In the spring of 1645, as a great scholar of the East Court and the minister of military affairs, Shi Kefa was put in charge of supervising the Jianghuai region and defending Yangzhou. The Qing Prince Yu Dodo had several letters sent to Shi Kefa, trying to persuade him to join the Qing rulers, but he refused to surrender. With few troops and no outside help, Shi Kefa was still able to encourage his soldiers and the Yangzhou people to defend the besieged city. After the fall of Yangzhou, he attempted suicide but was captured. Much impressed by Shi Kefa's loyalty as a general, Prince Yu Dodo called on him to surrender and promised him a high position. However, fearless of death, Shi Kefa refused resolutely and was thus killed at the age of 44. The Qing forces then began the ten-day massacre in Yangzhou, known as Yangzhou's Ten Days in history. Afterwards, since Shi Dewei, his adopted son, couldn't find his body, he had to bury Shi Kefa's clothes and some of his belongings on the Plum Blossom Hill to the north of the city.

The Xiang Hall is the main building of the Shi Kefa Memorial Hall. At the front of the hall there is a very famous couplet: "When I see the plum blossoms, I seem to see the tears shed for the disappearance of my home country; and when I see the moonlight, the ministers from the former dynasty can still feel the strength of the country." The statue of Shi Kefa sits in the middle of the Xiang Hall, behind which lies the tomb of Shi Kefa.

Behind the Plum Blossom Hill is the Qingxue Pavilion also known as the Yimo Hall, where calligraphy and writings of Shi Kefa are displayed, including his letters to Prince Duo Ergun, a letter home and some couplets.

To the west of the Xiang Hall is the Ancestral Temple of Shi Kefa, where there are portraits, shrines and memorial tablets of Shi Kefa and memorial tablets of other officials who sacrificed their lives for defending Yangzhou city. The ink rubbing of "In Praise of Loyal Martyr Shi Kefa" by Emperor Qianlong is also kept here.

第四章
博物概览

“烟花三月下扬州”，古往今来的游客，对于这座城市，感受最深的莫过于其深厚的文化底蕴。漫步于桃红柳绿的瘦西湖畔，听着栖灵塔上的风吹铜铃声，看着这座城市的砖砖瓦瓦，都能感受到历史的灵魂。

历史的烟云早已散去，难以计数的文化遗产无声地讲述着往昔的繁华，也成就了众多的博物馆。扬州中国雕版印刷博物馆、中国玉器博物馆、中国剪纸博物馆、“扬州八怪”纪念馆、扬州唐城遗址博物馆、扬州淮扬菜博物馆、扬州工艺美术馆等无不散发着独特的魅力。

2005年10月9日，由江泽民同志题写馆名的扬州中国雕版印刷博物馆及扬州博物馆新馆正式开馆，这座地标性的建筑，揭开了扬州打造“文化博览城”的序幕。扬州打造古代文化与现代文明交相辉映的文化博览城，在全国是首创。现在“文化博览城”已成为这座城市的核心词之一，这是扬州人对历史文化的自信表达。

Chapter IV

Overview of Yangzhou Museums

As a poem goes, "The best time to visit Yangzhou is in early spring, when it is misty with willows and flowers." Through the ages, what impresses the tourists the most has always been the abundant cultural treasures of Yangzhou. Wandering along the Slender West Lake, where the peaches blossom and the willows turn green, hearing the bells of the Qiling Pagoda swaying in the wind and looking at the bricks and tiles in the city, tourists can deeply feel the soul of history.

The past has become history, fading from our memory. However, countless cultural relics are the living testimonies of the city's proud and prosperous past, which is reflected in various museums with their unique charms, such as China Block Printing Museum at Yangzhou, China Jade Museum, China Paper-cutting Museum, Museum of the Eight Eccentric Artists of Yangzhou, Museum of the Ruins of Yangzhou City in the Tang Dynasty, Yangzhou Huaiyang Cuisine Museum, Yangzhou Arts and Crafts Gallery and so on.

China Block Printing Museum at Yangzhou and Yangzhou Museum, whose names were inscribed by Jiang Zemin, opened their doors to the public on October 9th, 2005. This landmark became the prelude of making Yangzhou a Cultural Expo City. Yangzhou is also leading the way throughout the whole country in transforming herself into a Cultural Expo City, where ancient culture and modern civilization mix. Now, Cultural Expo City has become one of the core values of Yangzhou city, which reflects Yangzhou people's confidence in their history and culture.

第一节　扬州博物馆

扬州博物馆与扬州中国雕版印刷博物馆（简称双博馆）联成一体，位于扬州新城西区的明月湖西侧，与扬州国际展览中心隔湖相望。双博馆的建筑风格独特，外观采用荷叶造型，使之与紧邻的湖滨地理环境相融合，实现建筑与自然的统一，反映了“和谐”的建筑理念，也抽象地反映了水的属性。这是扬州地方特色文化精神的提炼,体现了人与自然和谐统一、建筑与环境交融合一的设计理念。

· 扬州博物馆与扬州中国雕版印刷博物馆

扬州博物馆的历史最早可追溯到1951年建立的扬州文物馆及同年筹建的苏北博物馆。经过60多年的发展，现在的扬州双博馆大楼占地总面积5万平方米，分为东西两大区。西区为扬州博物馆新馆，东区为扬州中国雕版印刷博物馆，中部大厅将两馆连接起来，使整个建筑融为一体。

馆内设有扬州历史展馆、“扬州八怪”书画馆、国宝馆和古代雕刻艺术馆等八个展馆。展品上起新石器时代，下至晚清民初，以汉唐文物、明清文物和雕版版片为特色，其中元代的霁蓝釉白龙纹梅瓶为“镇馆之宝”。

扬州历史展馆

地处江淮平原东部的扬州，是中国古代南北水陆交通的枢纽和东西物流集散的都市。扬州城的故事，如澎湃的广陵潮，波澜迭起，连绵不绝。

Section One Yangzhou Museum

Situated on the west side of the Mingyue Lake in the western Xincheng District, facing Yangzhou International Exhibition Center across the lake, China Block Printing Museum at Yangzhou and Yangzhou Museum, also called Yangzhou Double Museum for short, are built under the same roof. As seen from outside, the unique architecture of Yangzhou Double Museum takes the shape of lotus leaves, blending perfectly with the lakeside environment, incorporating the natural scenery and reflecting the concept of architectural harmony as well as water properties in an abstract way. Its unique architectural form, which originates from Yangzhou local characteristics and cultural traditions, represents the unity and harmonious co-existence of man and nature, architecture and environment.

The predecessors of Yangzhou Museum were Yangzhou Historical Relic Studies Museum and Northern Jiangsu Museum, both established in 1951. After 60 years of development and growth, Yangzhou Double Museum now covers an area of 50,000 square meters, consisting of two adjacent buildings, connected by the central hall. The western part of the museum complex is Yangzhou Museum while the eastern part is China Block Printing Museum at Yangzhou.

In the museum there are eight exhibition halls, namely the Exhibition Hall of the Ancient Yangzhou, the Exhibition Hall of Calligraphy and Paintings by the Eight Eccentric Artists of Yangzhou, the Exhibition Hall of National Treasure and the Exhibition Hall of Ancient Artistic Carvings. Exhibits date from the Neolithic Age to the late Qing Dynasty. They feature cultural relics of the Han Dynasty and the Tang Dynasty, as well as cultural relics and block prints of the Ming and Qing Dynasties. Among the exhibits, the Treasure of the Museum is a glazed plum-blossom vase with a white dragon design against a blue background from the Yuan Dynasty.

The Exhibition Hall of the Ancient Yangzhou

Located in the eastern part of the Jianghuai Plain, Yangzhou was the hub of land and water communication between the North and the South, as well as the great metropolis of distribution between the East and the West in ancient China. The story of Yangzhou city is just like the surging tide of Guangling, with a series of salient highlights. The Exhibition Hall

· 广陵潮——扬州古代城市故事

扬州历史展馆共分为五大板块：“争霸中原筑邗城”，“煮海铸钱兴扬州”，“扬一益二繁华地”，“烽烟滚滚扬州路”，“富甲天下话扬州”。

基本陈列“广陵潮——扬州古代城市故事”，陈列面积2300平方米，展线长度580米，陈列文物856件。在陈列内容设计上采用信息组团、分级传播的最新设计理念。整个展览以江、河、海为依托，以汉、唐、清三个时期为重点，以扬州历史上五大城池为主线，构成一个清晰和谐的整体。以春秋邗城、汉广陵城、唐城、宋城和明清城的城市故事，简洁明快地勾勒出扬州历史发展的主线，也映衬着中国历史发展的大势。

整个陈列以柳树色为基调元素，表现“绿杨城廓是扬州”的文化特征。用古楠木色作为辅助色调，寓意扬州历史的深厚底蕴。

整个场馆的布置独特而富有变化，仿佛让人进入了时空隧道。

“扬州八怪”书画馆

该馆陈列面积约717.2平方米，包括“扬州八怪书画精品展”和“馆藏明清书画展”两个展区，陈列文物66件。“扬州八怪”因为不同于传统的创作风格和狂放不羁的处世行为而被当世视为“怪人”，但其喜闻乐见的书画

of the Ancient Yangzhou, which is divided into five theme parts, vividly tells visitors the stories of Yangzhou city: the Hancheng Built to Strive for Hegemony over the Central Plains; the Guangling City Founded to Develop Natural Resources; the Most Prosperous Region in the Country; Yangzhou in War Flames; Yangzhou, the Richest City under Heaven.

Here the basic display Tide of Guangling—Stories of the Ancient Yangzhou City covers an exhibition area of 2,300 square meters, 580 meters in length, showcasing 856 pieces of cultural relics. What deserves to be mentioned regarding the layout of the exhibits is that the latest design concept of information grouping and grading transmission has been adopted here. Set against the background of the riverscape and seascape and centered along the main line of the five cities in Yangzhou history, the whole exhibition presents a clear and harmonious overall arrangement, highlighting the Han, Tang and Qing Dynasties. The stories of the ancient Yangzhou in different eras (the Hancheng in the Spring and Autumn Period, the Guangling city in the Han Dynasty, the Yangzhou city in the Tang Dynasty, the Yangzhou city in the Song Dynasty and the Yangzhou city in the Ming and Qing Dynasties) briefly outline the chronological development of Yangzhou and reflect the tendency of China's development as well.

The color of willow green is applied to the entire display as the basic color so as to emphasize the characteristic "The green city is Yangzhou", while the color of Nanmu, serving as a supporting color, implies the profound history of Yangzhou.

In all, the layout of the exhibition hall is unique and rich in variety, making people feel as if they were wandering in the time tunnel.

The Exhibition Hall of Calligraphy and Paintings by the Eight Eccentric Artists of Yangzhou

The exhibition hall covers an area of about 717.2 square meters. With 66 cultural relics, the exhibition is split into two displays, the first featuring the masterpieces of painting and calligraphy collections of the Eight Eccentric Artists of Yangzhou and the second showcasing the calligraphic works and paintings during the Ming and Qing Dynasties. The term Eight Eccentric Artists of Yangzhou refers to a group of idiosyncratic artists, who rejected the orthodox ideas about painting and preferred a style deemed expressive and individualistic, and had unstrained personalities that defied the conventions of their time. What makes the art of the Eight Eccentrics outstanding is the perfect

题材，诗书画印的完美结合，却冲破中国传统文人画的层层束缚，给中国画坛带来缕缕新意。“馆藏明清书画展”所选展品多是与扬州密切相关的书画家的作品，与“扬州八怪精品展”的作品相得益彰。书画家们精湛的艺术作品反映了扬州画坛的人文荟萃和异彩纷呈，同时也展现了历史文化名城扬州丰厚的文化底蕴。

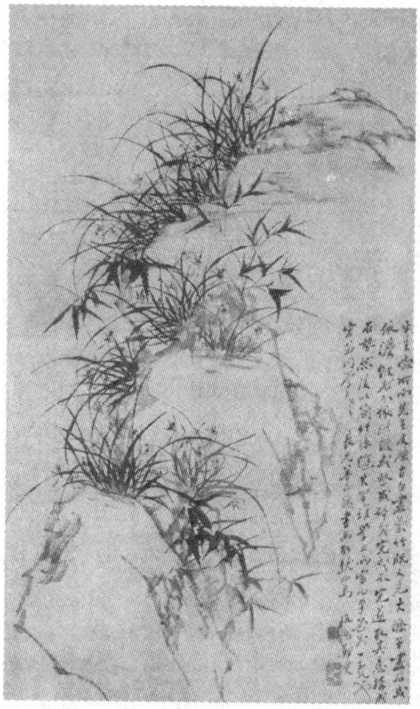

·郑板桥·兰竹石图轴

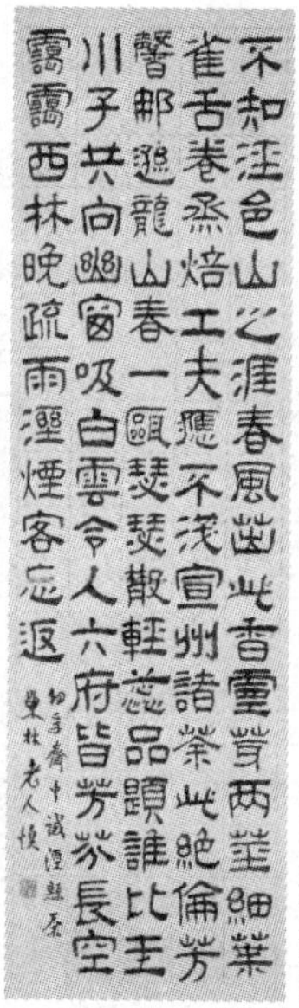

·汪士慎·隶书试泾县茶诗轴

·罗聘·唐人诗意图轴

国宝馆

该馆陈列面积184平方米，展厅仅陈列一件展品，即元霁蓝釉白龙纹梅瓶。该梅瓶属于元代景德镇窑蓝釉瓷器中的大型器物，造型秀美，蓝釉呈色鲜明纯正，腹部白龙环绕于瓶身，具有极强的艺术感染力，反映了元代景德镇窑的最高烧造水准。此种梅瓶目前传世仅见三件，一件为宫廷旧藏，现存北京颐和园；一件藏于法国巴黎吉美博物馆，两瓶都有残损；唯有扬州博物馆收藏的这件器型最大、纹饰最为精美，1992年被国家文物鉴定委员会评定为国宝级文物。

combination of poetry, calligraphy and painting in their works and new, experimental themes loved by the masses. The style of their paintings broke the conventions of the traditional Chinese artists and thus brought a refreshing novelty to Chinese paintings of that time. The Exhibition of Calligraphy and Paintings during the Ming and Qing Dynasties mostly displays the works of those artists closely associated with Yangzhou. The compositions and the fine works in the Exhibition of Calligraphy and Paintings by the Eight Eccentric Artists of Yangzhou contrast and complement each other. The artistic achievements of many a painter and calligrapher show that Yangzhou was once a gathering place for Chinese artists and a breeding ground for various styles of painting. At the same time, they firmly established Yangzhou as a famous historical and artistic city with a profound cultural foundation.

The Exhibition Hall of National Treasure

Covering an exhibition area of 184 square meters, the hall houses only one exhibit—a Yuan-dynasty sacrificial-blue glazed porcelain plum-blossom vase with a white dragon design. The vase is a large piece of blue glazed porcelain made in the Jingdezhen kiln during the Yuan Dynasty. This large vase possesses a strong aesthetic appeal and represents the highest level of porcelain-making techniques during the Yuan Dynasty. It is elegant in shape, the blue glaze is luminous and pure, and its belly is decorated with a white dragon design. Apart from the plum-blossom vase in Yangzhou Museum, there are two other examples of this vase around the world. One belongs to the royal collection and now is kept in the Summer Palace in Beijing, while the other is stored at Guimet Museum in France. However, those two vases have been somewhat damaged. The vase kept in Yangzhou Museum, which has the finest motif and is the biggest extant specimen of its kind and is in good condition, and was evaluated as the National Treasure in 1992 by the National Cultural Relics Appraisement Commission.

·国宝馆

·元·霁蓝釉白龙纹梅瓶

古代雕刻艺术馆

该馆陈列面积526平方米，陈列文物135件。根据材质不同，展出文物分为玉雕、石雕、砖雕、漆雕、骨雕等类，分别诠释了中国古代灿烂的雕刻艺术，其中多个种类如玉雕、漆雕、木雕、砖雕、核雕等，充分体现了古代能工巧匠的艺术造诣，表达出当时人们对美的理解和追求，具有鲜明的扬州地方特色。

·春秋·龙纹白玉璜

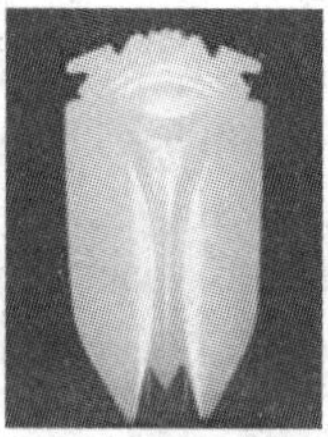

·西汉·白玉蝉

·明·龙纹石柱

The Exhibition Hall of Ancient Artistic Carvings

With 135 cultural relics on display, the hall covers about 526 square meters. In terms of raw materials, the exhibits come in many categories, such as carvings in jade, stone, brick, lacquer, bone and so on. These pieces illustrate the splendid ancient Chinese art of carving. Such examples as jade, lacquer, wood, brick and kernel carvings fully demonstrate the artistic achievements of ancient craftsmen and also embody the aesthetic understanding and pursuit of the Yangzhou people at that time. These carvings bear the most distinctive local features of Yangzhou.

第二节　扬州中国雕版印刷博物馆

印刷术被称为人类“文明之母”，中国的雕版印刷术被视为人类文明史上划时代的创造，在中国乃至世界印刷史上发挥过极为重要的作用。它出现于隋唐时期，距今已有1300多年的历史。

作为中国雕版印刷发祥地之一，扬州保存着极其丰富的雕版印刷文化遗产，其中雕版印刷技艺，被誉为“江苏一宝”、人类印刷史上的“活化石”，列入国家首批“非物质文化遗产名录”。扬州中国雕版印刷博物馆是中国唯一的一座雕版印刷博物馆，展厅总面积约4100平方米，分为中国馆与扬州馆两大部分，共陈列文物175件，全方位反映了中国雕版印刷的历史沿革及其在世界印刷史上产生的深远影响。

· 中国雕版印刷馆

中国馆

文字形成、笔墨纸的发明以及模印、捶拓、印花等技法为中国雕版印刷术的发明提供了物质基础和技术条件。隋唐之际，佛像、佛经以及民间生活用品如年历等的大量需求是雕版印刷产生的直接推动力。

雕版印刷工艺流程展区，通过生动的人物形象和综合表现手段，展现了从备料、写样、校正、上版、刻版、刷印到装帧的完整工艺流程，使参观者感受到雕版印刷不仅是技术,更是艺术。

Section Two China Block Printing Museum at Yangzhou

The art of printing has been called "the mother of civilization", and Chinese block printing is considered an epoch-making invention in the history of human civilization. Since its emergence, it has played an important role in the printing history of China and the world. Block printing appeared in the Sui and Tang Dynasties, with a history of over 1,300 years.

As one of the birthplaces of Chinese block printing, Yangzhou boasts a rich cultural heritage of block printing. The block printing technique, honored as A Treasure of Jiangsu Province and A Living Fossil in the history of block printing, was listed among the first batch of National Intangible Cultural Heritage. China Block Printing Museum at Yangzhou, with an exhibition hall of 4,100 square meters, is the only block printing museum in China. The museum displays 175 pieces of cultural relics and is divided into two major parts—China Pavilion and Yangzhou Pavilion. All of these comprehensively reflect the historical evolution of Chinese block printing and its far-reaching impacts on the history of world block printing.

China Pavilion

The formation of Chinese characters and the invention of writing brush, ink and paper, together with such techniques as sealing, rubbing, and printing, provided the material base and technical conditions for the emergence of block printing. What's more, during the Sui and Tang Dynasties, the large demand for Buddhist images, Buddhist sutras, and other necessities of daily life like calendars directly gave rise to the invention of block printing.

In the exhibition area of the technical process of block printing, the life-like sculptures and various comprehensive means of expression demonstrate to visitors the whole technical process of block printing, which includes selecting materials, writing the text on a piece of thin paper, proofreading, gluing the sheet face down onto a wooden plate, making a wood-block printing plate by engraving, printing and bookbinding. Here, visitors may feel that block printing is not only a technique but also an art form.

雕版印刷始于隋唐五代，盛于宋元时期，明清之际再度繁荣。形形色色的印刷物，在促进文字规范、民族团结、文明传承和满足社会发展需求方面发挥了巨大作用。

中国造纸术与印刷术在东西方的传播，不仅大大加速了文化传播，而且直接推动了一些地区的社会变革。

在中国馆中设置了一个雕版印刷演示互动区，以大空间、多视角、最鲜活的展示手法，全面介绍雕版工艺流程，观众既可以欣赏专业人员的高超技艺，又能够体验自己动手的乐趣。

·演示互动区

·游戏互动区

扬州馆

扬州的雕版刻书始于中唐，延续于宋、元、明，兴盛于清至民国，复兴于当代。时至今日，扬州中国雕版印刷博物馆尚存有10余万片珍贵的古籍版片，它们见证了古老雕版印刷工艺的发展历程。中华人民共和国成立后，为了弘扬中华民族优秀传统文化遗产，扬州成立了广陵古籍刻印社。该社成为全国惟一全面掌握纯手工的雕版印刷技艺并运用于古籍生产的单位，被誉为“江苏一宝”。

雕版古籍以其版本价值、收藏价值、工艺价值，深为海内外名家所欣赏，常作为国家领导人出访时的国礼，赠送给友好国家的首脑。2009年9月30日，联合国教科文组织保护非物质文化遗产政府间委员会第四次会议在阿联酋首都阿布扎比召开，会上作出决议，由扬州广陵古籍刻印社领衔、首次代表中国申报的雕版印刷技艺正式入选世界“人类非物质文化遗产代表作名录”。雕版印刷成为扬州市首个入选世遗的项目。

Block printing started in the Sui, Tang and Five Dynasties, prospered in the Song and Yuan Dynasties, and regained popularity in the Ming and Qing Dynasties. Undoubtedly, different types of prints have been playing a significant role in promoting language standardization, national unity, civilization inheritance and addressing social needs.

Furthermore, the spread of Chinese paper-making and printing in both Eastern and Western countries not only sped up the process of cultural communication, but also directly contributed to the social changes in some of those areas.

In China Pavilion, there is a large interactive demonstration area, where the most advanced presentation techniques and different angles of view are adopted to introduce the technological process of block printing. Here visitors can not only appreciate an amazing performance by a group of professionals, but also experience the pleasure of Do-It-Yourself in block printing.

Yangzhou Pavilion

The production of books by block printing in Yangzhou was first practiced in the middle of the Tang Dynasty and developed through the Song, Yuan and Ming Dynasties. It flourished from the Qing Dynasty to the Republic of China and has become prosperous again in modern times. Nowadays, the museum houses over 100,000 valuable ancient book blockings, which witnessed the development of the ancient block printing. After the founding of the People's Republic of China, to carry forward this excellent traditional heritage, Yangzhou established Guangling Ancient Book Block Printing House, which became well-known in China for its unique craftsmanship of using hand block printing technique in ancient book production. Owing to that, it is regarded as A Treasure of Jiangsu Province.

Block-printed ancient books are sought after and appreciated by collectors both at home and abroad, for they are of high edition, collection and artistic value. Besides, they are often presented as national gifts to foreign leaders. On September 30th, 2009, the fourth meeting of the Intergovernmental Committee of UNESCO for Safeguarding of the Intangible Heritage was held in Abu Dhabi, the United Arab Emirates. In the meeting, the technology of block printing represented by Guangling Ancient Book Block Printing House on behalf of China was officially awarded the title of Masterpiece of the Intangible Cultural Heritage of Humanity. Thus, block printing becomes the first project in Yangzhou that has been included in the list of World Intangible Cultural Heritage of Humanity.

第三节　“扬州八怪”纪念馆

“扬州八怪”纪念馆是扬州市政府于20世纪90年代为宣传和弘扬“扬州八怪”艺术成就而建的专业纪念馆，是利用“扬州八怪”之一金农曾寄居的西方寺古建筑群而建。纪念馆占地4452平方米，分陈列大厅、“扬州八怪”书画作品陈列室、金农寄居室等几部分，优美的园林景观与深厚的文化底蕴相得益彰。

·“扬州八怪”纪念馆

“扬州八怪”

“歌吹扬州惹怪名，兰香竹影伴书声”是邓拓同志咏叹清代著名画家郑燮(郑板桥)的诗句。这两句诗也形象地概括了由郑燮、金农、黄慎、李鳝、李方膺、汪士慎、高翔和罗聘所组成的“扬州八怪”的特点。他们中除高翔祖籍扬州，李鳝、郑燮是靠近扬州的兴化人外，其他人都是寄居在扬州。他们意气相投，关系密切，艺术上相互切磋，相互影响，在诗、书、画上形成了当时别具一格的风貌和情趣，人们习惯地称他们为“扬州八怪”。

·郑燮画像

“扬州八怪”知识广博，长于诗文，有相似的生活经历。他们大都历经坎坷，有的终生未入仕途，漂泊流浪，卖画为生；有的科举从政，一度出任小官，后被罢免或辞职，以卖画

Section Three The Memorial Hall of the Eight Eccentric Artists of Yangzhou

The Memorial Hall of the Eight Eccentric Artists of Yangzhou was specially set up by the Yangzhou municipal government in the 1990s to preserve and popularize the artistic achievements of the Eight Eccentric Artists of Yangzhou. The memorial hall was built on the site of the Xifang Temple, an ancient building complex which used to be the residence of Jin Nong—one of the Eight Eccentric Artists of Yangzhou. The hall covers an area of 4,452 square meters and consists of several parts, including the Exhibition Hall, the Exhibition Hall of Calligraphy and Paintings by the Eight Eccentric Artists of Yangzhou and Jin Nong's Former Residence. Here, the beautiful garden landscape and the profound cultural heritage complement each other.

The Eight Eccentric Artists of Yangzhou

Deng Tuo, a contemporary poet, once wrote a poem to eulogize Zheng Xie (Zheng Banqiao), a celebrated Chinese painter of the Qing Dynasty. The first two lines go like this: "Being called eccentric for his unconventional art work, with orchid flagrance, bamboo shadows and literature scrolls, he lived tastefully." The two lines also give us a general impression of the artistic styles and personalities of the Eight Eccentric Artists of Yangzhou, namely Zheng Xie, Jin Nong, Huang Shen, Li Shan, Li Fangying, Wang Shishen, Gao Xiang and Luo Pin. Among them, Gao Xiang was a native of Yangzhou; Li Shan and Zheng Xie were from Xinghua, a county-level city adjacent to Yangzhou; while the others sojourned in Yangzhou to make a living. They were on good terms with each other, sharing common characteristics in life and art, exchanging their ideas about art and inspiring each other. They gradually developed their unique styles in composing poems, writing calligraphy and painting. However, their works were considered odd at that time. Thus, they were named the Eight Eccentric Artists of Yangzhou.

The Eight Eccentric Artists of Yangzhou were a group of knowledgeable intellectuals, all of whom were highly skilled at poetry, calligraphy and painting. They had similar life experiences and most of them underwent a lot of hardships in their lives. Some of them never had the chance to be government officials, moving from place to place and selling their paintings to earn a living. Some were successful in passing the highest imperial examination and were appointed as petty

为继。沉闷时代的窒息，郁郁不得志的痛苦，迫使他们在艺术作品中抒发情感，从而在艺坛别具一格，独领风骚。他们凭着知识分子的敏锐洞察力和悲天悯人的情怀，对丑恶的事物和人加以抨击，或著于诗文，或表诸书画，以书画寄情，借助书画抒发内心的愤懑。他们的艺术大都取材花鸟，以写意为主要表现方式，但书画艺术不受正宗的成法和古法的束缚，打破当时的僵化局面，在继承传统的基础上革新、创造与发挥，不同于古人，不追随时俗，风格独创。他们从大自然中发掘灵感，从生活中寻找题材，下笔自成一家，达到了立意新、构图新、技法新的境界，开创了一代新画风。

“扬州八怪”的大胆创新之风，不断为后世画家所传承。近现代名画家如王小梅、吴让之、齐白石、徐悲鸿、黄宾虹、潘天寿等，都各自在某些方面受“扬州八怪”作品的影响。徐悲鸿曾在郑燮的一幅《兰竹》画上题字：“板桥先生为中国近三百年最卓绝的人物之一。其思想奇，文奇，书画尤奇。观其诗文及书画，不但想见高致，而其寓仁悲于奇妙，尤为古今天才之难得者。”

“扬州八怪”不仅给我们后代留下了很多珍贵的墨宝，更是对中国绘画的发展立下了不朽的功劳。“扬州八怪”成为中国文化史上的一个重要现象，也是扬州文化史上的一大亮点。

officials; but had to resign or were dismissed later because of offending higher officials. Afterwards, they went back home and made a living by painting. Suffering from the suffocating control of that time and the misunderstanding of their art by the conventional contemporary artists, they rejected the orthodox ideas about painting and sought their own style, deemed expressive, creative and unique. Since they lived close to the lower-class people, they were aware of the decadence and corruption of the society and the suffering of the people. Their keen perception of the society, their resentment and anger at its ugly side and their sympathy for the ordinary people were reflected in their poems, calligraphy and paintings. Their paintings mostly adopted the subject of flowers and birds in *xieyi* (depicting the idea) style. In all, their art broke away from the orthodox school of painting and the rigid format of the old brushstroke conventions. Following the tradition in their artistic pursuit, they developed their unique painting styles. Instead of adhering to the conventionally-accepted manners, they drew inspiration from nature and subject from life. Their paintings are distinctively characterized by their creativity and individuality in terms of conception, composition and technique. Thus, the revolutionary painting school of the Eight Eccentric Artists of Yangzhou came into being. They opened a new era in Chinese painting history.

The bold and innovative style of the eight artists' paintings has greatly influenced and inspired countless great painters of later generations, such as famous modern and contemporary masters Wang Xiaomei, Wu Rangzhi, Qi Baishi, Xu Beihong, Huang Binhong and Pan Tianshou. Xu Beihong once wrote an inscription on Zheng Xie's representative painting Orchid and Bamboo, "Mr. Zheng Banqiao is one of the most outstanding figures in China in the recent 300 years. He is famous for his unique ideas and poems, and especially his calligraphy works and paintings. His poems, calligraphy works and paintings reflect not only creative thinking and unyielding temperament, but also originality by merging kindness and compassion into creatively arranged compositions. He was indeed a rare genius."

The Eight Eccentric Artists of Yangzhou left us a great number of precious art works. More importantly, they made a great contribution to the development of Chinese painting. The Eight Eccentric Artists of Yangzhou have become an important cultural phenomenon in the history of Chinese culture and a highlight in the cultural history of Yangzhou.

陈列大厅

"扬州八怪"雕像

陈列大厅原为西方寺的大殿，是明代洪武年间（1368-1398年）的建筑，雕梁画栋至今色彩艳丽。大厅内有15位代表人物的塑像，并介绍了"扬州八怪"产生的时代背景以及他们的生平事迹和各自特长。

"扬州八怪"书画作品陈列室

东西廊房陈列有"扬州八怪"书画（复制品），表现每位书画家的个性创作；精品陈列室陈列着"扬州八怪"传人李亚如的画作精品。近六十幅的"扬州八怪"书画刻石，再现了中国传统碑刻的神韵。

·黄慎·见福图

·李鳝·五松图

·李亚如·凌霄

金农寄居室

"扬州八怪"诸家中，金农是领衔人物，他领异标新，艺术上追求古拙奇异。这位杰出的艺术大师，一生奔波，穷困潦倒，晚年流落扬州，借宿扬州的西方寺。很难想象，一无所有、在窘境中挣扎的金农，会有《荷塘忆旧图》这样的闲情小品。荷花铺满画卷，清新明丽。荷叶连接碧水远天，长廊，栏杆，空寂无人，却分明觉得有伊人的倩影。画面含蓄隽永，有一缕温馨的气息在弥漫。

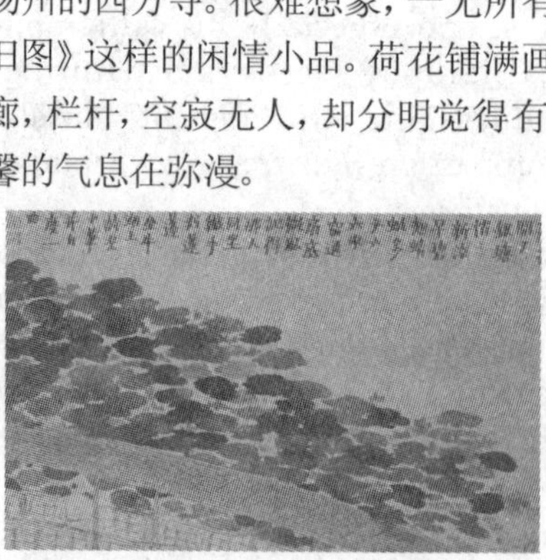

·金农·《荷塘忆旧图》

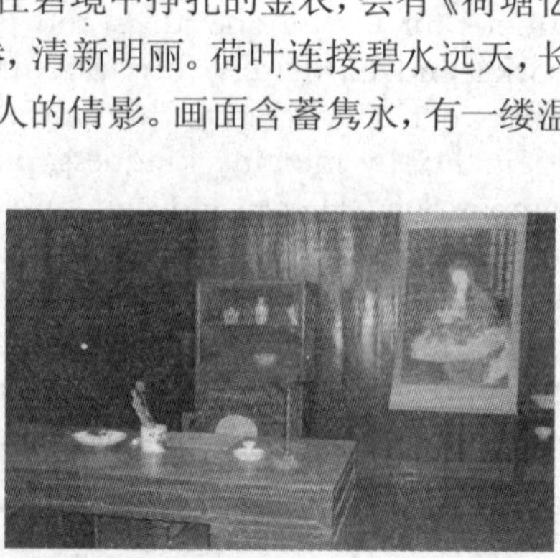

·金农寄居室

The Exhibition Hall

The Exhibition Hall was once the main hall of the Xifang Temple, and was built during the Hongwu Period (1368-1398) in the Ming Dynasty. The temple has elaborately carved pillars and painted beams, whose bright and beautiful colors have remained almost the same over time. The hall houses fifteen statues of different artists, including the Eight Eccentric Artists of Yangzhou, as well as the introduction of their backgrounds, life stories and their specialties.

The Exhibition Hall of Calligraphy and Paintings by the Eight Eccentric Artists of Yangzhou

The eight artists' paintings and calligraphy (replica) are displayed in the eastern and western halls, showing every artist's individual artistic style. The Exhibition Hall of Selected Works displays a fine array of the masterpieces by Li Yaru, a successor of the Eight Eccentric Artists of Yangzhou. What's more, nearly 60 stone inscriptions of paintings and calligraphic works by the Eighte Eccentric Artists of Yangzhou are exhibited here to reflect the charm of traditional Chinese inscriptions on stone tablets.

Jin Nong's Former Residence

Jin Nong was the most famous among the Eight Eccentric Artists of Yangzhou. The style of his paintings was unorthodox, simple and eccentric. Living a poor life, this outstanding artist had to move from place to place all his life. Later, due to poverty, he had to spend his later years in the Xifang Temple in Yangzhou. Though he always had financial difficulties, he was blessed with a rich inner life. Take his painting Memory of Lotus Pond for example, it is difficult to imagine how he created such an elegant composition with a remarkably fresh atmosphere when he was struggling to survive. The painting features a pond dotted with lotus leaves and flowers densely huddled together. Lotus leaves stand out boldly above the clear water, stretching far into the sky and getting connected to the long corridor and railings. There is nobody to be seen, but it gives viewers an impression that a beauty is somewhere in the painting. The painting appears fresh, implicit and meaningful, creating a warm atmosphere.

第四节　扬州中国盆景博物馆

中国的盆景艺术，主要有五大流派，即“扬（扬州）派、苏（苏州）派、川（成都）派、岭南（广州）派和海（上海）派”。扬派盆景形式别致、层次分明，严整平稳，犹如中国绘画艺术之工笔细描。相比川派、苏派、岭南派和海派，扬派盆景古老的剪扎技艺保存最为完整。2008年6月，扬派盆景技艺入选国家“非物质文化遗产名录”，这是扬派盆景技艺传承与发展的里程碑，具有划时代的意义。

扬派盆景在唐代已有流传。苏东坡在扬州任太守时，除吟诗作画外，更喜欢制作盆景，并对入画的盆景加以吟咏：“我持此石归，袖中有东海。……置之盆盎中，日与山海对。”到了清代，扬州广建园林，大兴盆景，有“家家有花园，户户养盆景”之说，并形成流派。李斗所著的《扬州画舫录》中曾提到，乾隆年间，扬州有花树点景和山水点景，还有做成瀑布的盆景。郑板桥的题画《盆梅》，更形象地展示了当时的梅花盆景艺术。

扬州盆景分树桩盆景、山水盆景和水旱盆景等。其中观叶类的树桩盆景，可谓独树一帜。由于受扬州明清时期画风的熏陶，以及古城造园、养花传统的影响，扬派盆景形成了自己独特的风格。它仿效名山大川，借鉴山水名画，造型严谨而富有变化，清秀而不失壮观。

·腾云

Section Four China Potted Landscape Museum at Yangzhou

Chinese potted landscapes generally fall into five categories according to the region of their origin, namely the Yang (Yangzhou) school, Su (Suzhou) school, Chuan (Chengdu) school, Southern Ridge (Guangzhou) school, and Hai (Shanghai) school. Just like the Chinese traditional painting with meticulous detail, the Yangzhou bonsai is characterized by a unique shape and clearly defined layers of branches, best expressing serenity and neatness. Compared with the other four schools, the ancient skills of cutting and tying have been preserved most completely in the Yang school. In June 2008, Yangzhou bonsai art was included in the National Intangible Cultural Heritage List, which was both an epoch-making event and a milestone in the inheritance and development of this art form.

By the Tang Dynasty, bonsai was widespread and had begun to interest the public in Yangzhou. Su Dongpo, one of the top poets in the Song Dynasty, enjoyed composing poetry and painting, as well as bonsai-making in his spare time when he was prefect in Yangzhou. He wrote a poem about a beautiful potted landscape that he painted: "One day I return from the sea with a pretty stone; my sleeve contains the Eastern Sea ... Put it in the pot, and the seas and mountains are unfolding in front of me." The Qing Dynasty witnessed rapid development in the Yangzhou garden landscaping and bonsai-making. Therefore, the following saying became popular then: "Every household has a garden, and every family grows bonsais." It was during the same period that different schools of bonsais came into being. Li Dou mentions the bonsais in his *Pleasure Boats of Yangzhou*: during the reign of Emperor Qianlong, there are flower-and-tree bonsai, landscape bonsai and the cascade-type bonsai in Yangzhou. Zheng Banqiao also vividly depicted the potted prunus mume in his painting with an inscription Potted Prunus Mume.

The Yangzhou bonsai is mainly divided into three categories—tree stumps, landscape, and water and land. Among them, the Yangzhou tree-stump bonsais, featuring ornamental foliage layers, are in a class of their own. Inspired by the painting styles during the Ming and Qing Dynasties, as well as the tradition of lanscaping gardens after natural scenery and growing flowers in the old city of Yangzhou, Yangzhou bonsai has developed its unique style. Since the art of Yangzhou bonsai-making seeks to imitate famous mountains and great rivers and draw

1980年4月16日至5月6日，日本举行了国际盆景水石展览会，其间在大阪召开了第一届世界盆栽会议。扬州盆景艺术作为中国唯一的代表参展，中国盆景艺术大师赵庆泉在会上作了《中国盆景艺术的悠久历史及其独特风格》的发言，引起了强烈的国际反响。1985年，“中国盆景评比展览”在上海举行，全国60多个城市参展，扬州送展53盆，其中12盆获奖，获奖总数居全国之冠。扬派盆景一代宗师万觐棠的代表作《巧云》、《瑞云》、《翠云》等，不但在国内各大型盆景展览评比中屡次夺魁，而且饮誉海外，在世界盆景界引起震动，其作品远销英国、日本、德国、丹麦、荷兰等国。

· 一代盆景宗师万觐棠

为更好地发展盆景艺术，2000年4月，扬州市设立了扬州中国盆景博物馆，分为东馆（红园）和西馆（盆景园）。扬州中国盆景博物馆内保存着历届获奖作品，不仅有现代盆景，还保存着40多盆古盆景。园内除树桩盆景外，还陈列大量水石盆景，在全国盆景界享有极高声誉。

2009年，扬州中国盆景博物馆的扬派盆景移至瘦西湖公园万花园中的扬派盆景艺术博物馆，为瘦西湖增添了一道亮丽的风景。

· 扬州中国盆景博物馆（西馆）

inspiration from great landscape paintings, it is not surprising that the Yangzhou bonsai displays a pleasing balance of meticulous shaping and rich variation, as well as a unique blend of elegance and grandeur.

The First World Bonsai Convention was held in Osaka during the World Bonsai and Suiseki Exhibition, which ran from April 16 to May 6, 1980. The Yangzhou bonsai was invited to the exhibition as the only representative of bonsai from China. At the convention, Zhao Qingquan, one of the best-known Chinese bonsai masters, made a speech named "The Chinese Bonsai Art—Its Long History and Unique Styles", which received a quite positive response internationally. In 1985, the first Chinese National Bonsai Exhibition was held in Shanghai, with more than 60 cities in China participating in this judged exhibition. Fifty-three bonsai exhibits from Yangzhou were on display, twelve of which won prizes. Yangzhou ranked first in the whole nation in terms of total medals. The bonsai masterpieces, Qiaoyun (Ingenious or Delicate Clouds), Ruiyun (Good Luck Clouds), and Cuiyun (Green Clouds) were all made by Wan Jintang, a world-famous Chinese bonsai master. Each time these art works were taken to the large-scale bonsai exhibitions in China, they took first prizes and earned him wide praise from bonsai artists and collectors all over the world. His works also found their way to the markets in Britain, Japan, Germany, Denmark, the Netherlands and other countries.

To further develop the Chinese bonsai art, in April 2000, Yangzhou established China Potted Landscape Museum at Yangzhou, which consists of the East Hall (the Red Garden) and the West Hall (the Potted Landscape Garden). Within the gardens are the award-winning bonsai masterpieces, some modern potted landscapes, and more than 40 pieces of potted landscapes survived from ancient times. Some tree-stump potted landscapes as well as large numbers of Suiseki bonsais are also exhibited here. Owing to these potted landscapes, China Potted Landscape Museum at Yangzhou enjoys a high reputation in China.

In 2009, the bonsais of China Potted Landscape Museum at Yangzhou found a new home in the Yangzhou-style Potted Landscape Museum, which is situated in the Multicolored Garden of the Slender West Lake Park, adding more charm to the Slender West Lake Scenic Spot.

第五章
美食品赏

扬州自古就被誉为“东方浪漫之都”，其文化内涵非常丰富。其中，美食文化就有着源远流长的历史，无论是淮扬菜肴，还是面点小吃、扬州酱菜，都有着令人赞叹的色、香、味。

·蟹粉狮子头

·扬州炒饭

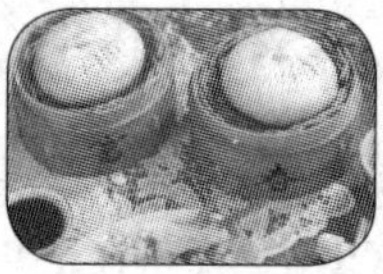
·富春面点

·四美酱菜

扬州是中国四大菜系之一淮扬菜的发祥地。淮扬菜是中国烹饪技艺最高水平的代表之一，它在众多菜系中独树一帜，素有“东南第一佳味”、“天下之至美”之誉。2001年7月，扬州被中国烹饪协会授予“中国淮扬菜之乡”的称号，成为中国烹饪协会正式命名的第一个菜系之乡。淮扬菜系始于春秋，兴于汉唐，盛于明清。在文化层面上形成了“高雅、精致、融和、时尚、养生”的基本元素，在技术层面上形成了“选料严格、制作精细，注重火候、擅长炖焖，清淡味醇、咸甜适中，造型优美、色泽雅丽”的风格。

Chapter V

Appreciation of Yangzhou Cuisine

Thanks to its exceedingly rich cultural connotation, Yangzhou has been well-known as A Romantic City in the East since ancient times. As part of Yangzhou culture, Yangzhou cuisine is best known for its long history. Huaiyang cuisine, pastry and snacks, and Yangzhou pickles all have an appealing combination of color, aroma and taste.

As one of the four major Chinese cuisines, Huaiyang cuisine originated in Yangzhou. As one of the highest level representatives in Chinese cooking skills, Huaiyang cuisine enjoys the reputation of Superior Taste in Southeast China and the Most Delicious Dishes in the World. In July 2001, Yangzhou was awarded the title Home to Chinese Huaiyang Cuisine by China Cuisine Association, and became the first city to receive such honor. Huaiyang cuisine appeared in the Spring and Autumn Period, developed in the Han and Tang Dynasties, and flourished in the Ming and Qing Dynasties. Culturally speaking, Yangzhou cuisine features a combination of elegance, delicacy, integration, fashion, and health. Technically speaking, Yangzhou cuisine has the characteristics of carefully selected ingredients, exquisite workmanship, stewing and braising with perfect timing, light and mellow flavors, moderate saltiness and sweetness, elegant form and fresh colors.

第一节 扬州名宴

扬州是淮扬菜的发源地和中心。淮扬菜见于文献，当自《尚书》“淮海惟扬州”始。自先秦发展至汉晋，史载扬州已是“熟食遍列”。隋唐、明清尤见繁盛。特别是大运河开凿以后，扬州成为盐漕两运、物资集散和中外进出口贸易的水陆交通枢纽，经济发达，为淮扬菜系的发展打下了坚实的基础。除此之外，扬州地处鱼米之乡，气候适宜，物产丰富。描述此类事物的词句更是比比皆是。如苏东坡《扬州以土物寄少游》提及的鲜鲫、紫蟹、姜芽、鸭蛋，郑板桥诗词中描述的鲜笋、鲥鱼和“蒲筐包蟹、竹笼装虾、柳条穿鱼”等，海味产区亦近在咫尺。这样背景下孕育的淮扬菜，文化积淀深厚，因而，很早就确立了中华一大风味菜系的地位。

· 开国第一宴（部分）

1949年10月1日中华人民共和国成立，开国大典当晚，北京饭店承办了新中国的第一次国宴，由淮扬菜厨师承担。毛泽东、刘少奇、周恩来等党和国家领导人、外宾等共600多人出席，自此“开国第一宴”更使淮扬菜名扬天下。

Section One Famous Banquets of Yangzhou

Since the ancient times, Yangzhou has been the cradle and center of Huaiyang cuisine. The earliest known record relating to Huaiyang cuisine can be found in *The Book of History*, "The Huai and the sea formed the boundaries of Yangzhou." Huaiyang cuisine can be traced to the Pre-Qin Period, and it enjoyed rapid development during the Han and Jin Dynasties, which is testified in the historical records, "Cooked food stalls can be seen everywhere in town." Later on, the Sui, Tang, Ming and Qing Dynasties witnessed the greatest prosperity of Huaiyang cuisine. Due to the construction of the Grand Canal during the Sui Dynasty, Yangzhou became a water and land transportation hub for salt and grain, a distribution center and a prominent import and export harbor, enjoying economic prosperity. Besides its convenient transportation, Yangzhou, long known as a land of fish and rice, benefits from favorable climate and abundant resources. All of these factors laid a solid foundation for the development of Huaiyang cuisine. There are numerous poems and articles dedicated to Yangzhou specialties. While Su Dongpo was a governor of Yangzhou, he wrote to a contemporary poet Qin Shaoyou the poem titled *Sending Specialties of Yangzhou to Shaoyou*, in which he made a detailed record of Yangzhou local delicacies of that time, like fresh crucian carps, purple crabs, ginger buds and duck eggs. Zheng Banqiao also depicted Yangzhou's local products in many of his literary works, such as "fresh bamboo shoots, reeves shads, crabs in calamus bags, shrimps in bamboo cages and fish strung on wickers". Yangzhou lies within easy reach of coastal towns, so sea ingredients are not hard to find in Huaiyang cuisine. Developed and steeped under such circumstances, Huaiyang cuisine has a rich cultural foundation. Therefore, it has long been one of China's four major cuisines.

On the founding day of the People's Republic of China, October 1, 1949, the First State Banquet, a part of the founding ceremony, was held in Beijing Hotel. The banquet featured Huaiyang dishes. On that evening, more than 600 people attended the banquet, including Party and State leaders Mao Zedong, Liu Shaoqi, Zhou Enlai, other founders of the People's Republic of China and some foreign guests. Thanks to the First State Banquet, Huaiyang cuisine has been enjoying a worldwide fame ever since then.

时至今日，淮扬菜系更是名厨辈出，高手如林。他们不仅继承、发扬了淮扬菜的优良传统，而且深谙创新是发展之灵魂、兴盛之动力的道理，创出了闻名遐迩的“红楼宴”、“乾隆御宴”等系列菜品。2009年，中国烹饪协会正式授予扬州迎宾馆的“红楼宴”、“满汉全席”和“乾隆御宴”、扬州会议中心的“烟花三月宴”、扬州西园大酒店的“秋瑞宴”和“红楼早宴”、扬州康山园的“卢氏家宴”、扬州宾馆的“‘扬州八怪’宴”、扬州花园国际大酒店的“三头宴”和“春晖宴”为“中国名宴”。十大名宴的创立，对于推动淮扬菜乃至中国饮食文化的发展有着重要作用。

红楼宴

《红楼梦》诞生于18世纪中叶，它既是体现满汉文化、南北文化相互碰撞、吸收融合的典范，又是中国明末清初时期贵族生活的真实写照。在这部名著中，曹雪芹用了将近三分之一的篇幅，描述了众多人物丰富多彩的饮食文化活动，通过各种各样的宴席，不仅为读者提供了一份富有特色的美食单，更重要的是为我们创造了一个完整的红楼饮食文化体系。

· 曹雪芹像

曹家在南京和扬州两地居住60多年，饮食多为淮扬风味。小说《红楼梦》以“声色饮馔之幻”来演示人生哲理，作者对淮扬烹饪文化素材

· 红楼宴

So far, premier chefs and masters of Huaiyang cuisine have come forth in great numbers. Knowing well that innovation is the soul of advancement and the driving power of prosperity, they carry on and develop the traditional culinary art of Huaiyang cuisine. By now, they have created a large assortment of well-known dishes, like the Red Mansion Banquet and the Imperial Banquet of Emperor Qianlong. In 2009, China Cuisine Association officially approved and granted Yangzhou ten famous feasts in the title of Chinese Famous Feasts, namely, the Red Mansion Banquet, the Manchu Han Imperial Feast, and the Imperial Banquet of Emperor Qianlong presented by Yangzhou State Guesthouse, the Feast of Misty Flowers of March by Yangzhou Convention Center, the Auspicious Autumn Feast and the Red Mansion Breakfast by Yangzhou West Garden Hotel, the Lu Family Feast by Yangzhou Kangshan Garden, the Banquet of the Eight Eccentric Artists of Yangzhou by Yangzhou Hotel, the Three Head Banquet and the Chunhui Feast by Yangzhou Garden International Hotel. These ten famous Chinese feasts have played an important role in promoting Huaiyang cuisine as well as Chinese food culture.

The Red Mansion Banquet

A Dream of the Red Mansions (one of China's Four Great Classics) was composed in the middle of the 18th century during the Qing Dynasty. This novel is a paradigm with great cultural richness, where the Manchu and Han cultures, as well as the cultures of North China and South China, are brought together, blending and merging with each other. Besides, it vividly portrays the daily life of the upper class in the late Ming and early Qing Dynasties. In this masterpiece, its author, Cao Xueqin, spared nearly one third of the novel to describe in detail the rich dietetic cultures of its characters. The novel depicts a variety of family feasts, grand banquets and small feasts, which presents readers not only an elaborate menu of delicacies, but also a complete system of Red Mansion Cuisine.

The Cao family (Cao Xueqin, his father and forefathers) took residence in Nanjing and Yangzhou for more than 60 years, making the family kitchen mainly Huaiyang style. "The illusions of feasting, drinking, music and dancing" described in *A Dream of the Red Mansions* actually allude to life philosophy. The readers are amazed that Cao Xueqin was so familiar with Huaiyang cuisine and cooking ingredients that he could

驾轻就熟，信手拈来皆成文章，令人叹为观止。曹雪芹的家庭与扬州有着深厚的历史渊源，因此，扬州烹饪文化界对于红楼宴的开发责无旁贷。

满汉全席

满汉全席是我国一种具有浓郁民族特色的巨型宴席，一直被推崇为中国宴席的经典之作。乾隆年间李斗所著的《扬州画舫录》中记有一份满汉全席食单，是关于满汉全席的最早记载。其他一些古籍也多有满汉全席的记载，它们为恢复满汉全席提供了较为详实的历史资料。

·满汉全席节选菜品

满汉全席其实并非源于宫廷，而是江南的官场菜。清代，康熙皇帝南巡，视察扬州，开始设满汉全席。乾隆皇帝六次南巡，扬州官绅接驾，仍沿承满汉全席。从此满汉全席声名远扬，各地竞相仿制。

满汉全席取材广泛，用料精细，山珍海味无所不包。满汉全席的菜点精美，礼仪讲究，形成了引人注目的独特风格。完整的满汉全席有134道热菜、48道冷荤及各种点心、干鲜果品，分四至六餐食完。南北风味之精华，

readily write poems and articles about them. Since Yangzhou and Cao Xueqin's family were closely connected to each other, the culinary people, catering business operators, and scholars engaged in Yangzhou catering industry are bound to study and develop the dishes of the Red Mansion Banquet described in the novel.

The Manchu Han Imperial Feast

In Chinese history, the Manchu Han Imperial Feast (the royal feast of the Qing Dynasty with desserts of Manchu ethnic group and dishes of Han ethnic group) is a grand and luxurious feast with rich ethnic characteristics, which has been recommended as the classic Chinese banquet since its appearance. The earliest records containing the complete menu and recipes of Manchurian and Chinese delicacies can be found in *Pleasure Boats of Yangzhou* written by Li Dou during the Qianlong reign of the Qing Dynasty. Detailed descriptions of the feast, the dishes, and ingredients are also available in some other ancient books. All of these detailed historical records contributed to the revival of the complete Manchu Han Imperial Feast.

Actually, the dishes of the Manchu Han Imperial Feast originated from the meals in the official circles in South China instead of the imperial court's kitchen. It is said that during the reign of Emperors Kangxi and Qianlong in the Qing Dynasty, the dishes of the Manchu Han Imperial Feast were, in the beginning, offered by the local officials of Yangzhou to entertain emperors and senior officials from the imperial court. According to historical records, when Emperor Kangxi went on his southern inspection tours, the local officials of Yangzhou entertained him with the Manchu Han Imperial Feast. Emperor Qianlong also visited South China six times. Yangzhou officials entertained him with the Manchu Han Imperial Feast each time. Since then, the dishes have become known far and wide and were imitated everywhere.

The Manchu Han Imperial Feast features a wide range of fine ingredients that include delicacies from mountain and sea, which are carefully chosen and prepared. The feast is characterized by its abundant and exquisite dishes, its elaborate meal service and fine dining etiquettes, creating its own charm in Chinese cuisine. The complete Manchu Han Imperial Feast contains 134 hot dishes, 48 cold ones, various kinds of refreshments and pastries, as well as dried and fresh fruits. It is such a grand feast that it is divided into four to six meals. Undoubtedly, the complete Manchu Han Imperial Feast is the treasure and the finest

蔚为大观，既有满人的豪放，又有汉人的细腻，是中华菜系文化的瑰宝和最高境界。

为了使满汉全席从历史中走出来，扬州烹饪界的专家、学者殚精竭虑，对满汉全席重新进行设计。现在，全席分两套，每套菜肴108道。为了给品尝者提供较大的选择余地，有三日六宴、两日四宴、一日两宴、精品宴等四种模式。每宴菜肴36款，席间“满”与“汉”的菜点交替呈现，使就餐者领略“中和”饮食文化的韵味。

乾隆御宴

清朝乾隆皇帝在位60年，期间六次南巡，每次南巡都以在扬州停留的时间最长。所到之处，珍肴美食，莫不遍尝。乾隆南巡行程多在仲春至初夏，乾隆御宴原料以春夏江鲜为主，辅以河鲜、蔬鲜，配以名特产品，形成了“高、精、素、补”的风格。

· 乾隆御宴

为了让珍贵精美的宫廷宴重新焕发光彩，扬州迎宾馆的师傅们参照清代《扬州画舫录》、《随园食单》等书籍，坚持“力求御宴原貌，突显宫廷特色，注重养生理念，挖掘文化内涵”的创意原则，从记载的近百款乾隆御宴珍肴中，反复推敲，再三筛选，并以此为基础采用现代烹调方法，汲取地方风味菜肴特色，不断完善，推出了面目一新的“乾隆御宴”。

expression of Chinese cuisine, which is a perfect combination of different flavors from South and North China, the bold and unconstrained character of the Manchu people and the subtle and refined style of the Han people.

In order to reproduce the Manchu Han Imperial Feast according to historical records, today the experts and scholars of Yangzhou catering industry have been working hard to rewrite the menu of the Manchu Han Imperial Feast and redesign its courses. The banquet is divided into two sets with 108 dishes in each. There are four modes, namely, six banquets in three days, four banquets in two days, two banquets in one day and a high quality banquet, which offers the diners a wide range of choices. Each banquet has 36 dishes. During the banquet, the Manchurian and Chinese dishes are presented alternately, so that the diners can fully appreciate the lasting appeal of the integral catering culture of China.

The Imperial Banquet of Emperor Qianlong

During his 60 year's reign, Emperor Qianlong completed six southern inspection tours. During his inspections, the emperor would spend the longest time in Yangzhou and taste various kinds of delicacies and snacks. In most cases, Emperor Qianlong would set out for his southern inspections in mid spring or early summer, when the river and sea foods are in season. The Imperial Banquet of Emperor Qianlong features the main ingredients of sea foods, along with river foods and vegetables in season, supplemented with specialties of Yangzhou. Thus, the banquet style can be summed up as "noble, exquisite, light-flavored and nutritious".

In order to revive the spirit of the precious and exquisite imperial banquets, the chefs of Yangzhou State Guesthouse referred to the books written in the Qing Dynasty, like *Pleasure Boats of Yangzhou* and *The Menu of Sui Garden*. Adhering to the innovative principles of "striving to keep the original flavor of royal dishes, highlighting the characteristics of the imperial court, attaching great importance to healthy diet, exploiting the connotation of food culture", they studied and pondered over the records of nearly one hundred royal dishes of Emperor Qianlong. After the above research, they adopted the modern cooking method, incorporated the distinct flavors of classic specialties, continued to perfect the banquet from its original form, and finally developed the new Imperial Banquet of Emperor Qianlong.

第二节　扬州名点

· 扬州早茶

“扬州好，茶社客堪邀。加料干丝堆细缕，熟铜烟袋卧长苗，烧酒水晶肴。”这首清词是扬州人惬意生活的生动写照。扬州的早晨，因为有了各种精致的淮扬早点，而变得更加丰富和恬然。

淮扬名点以制作精巧、造型讲究、馅心多样、各具特色而著称。至明清时代已是“扬郡面馆，美甲天下。”《望江南百调》中称：“淮扬点心，清鲜与甘甜搭配，荤腥与蔬菜组合，蓬松与柔韧相辅，酥脆与绵软对成，养荣伞面，口感美好，富有回味，而且形态小巧玲珑使人喜爱。”来扬州品尝过淮扬点心的各地美食家无不交口称赞。

制作淮扬名点的大师中，最负盛名的当数清代中期仪征的萧美人，她制作的面点在当时可谓价比黄金。清代著名文学家、美食家袁枚在《随园食单》记载：“仪征南门外，萧美人擅制点心，凡馒头、糕点之类，小巧可爱，洁白如雪。”当代中国餐饮界将她列为中国古代十大名厨之一。近现代扬州点心大师有尹长山、张广庆、董德安、陈恩德等，其中陈恩德大师继承传统，古为今用、

· 富春茶社

Section Two Famous Snacks and Refreshments of Yangzhou

"Yangzhou is wonderful! The teahouse is a popular place for local people to entertain their important visitors. Piled on the plate are dried tofu threads marinated in savory ingredients; here copper hookahs with bamboo pipes are waiting to be served too; crystal meat is a perfect match for alcohol." This poem of the Qing Dynasty describes the leisure activities among Yangzhou residents. In Yangzhou, various kinds of snacks and refreshments make each morning a pleasant one.

For many years, Yangzhou snacks and refreshments have been well known for their great variety with different fillings, exquisite workmanship and elegant shape. By the Ming and Qing Dynasties, Yangzhou city was praised as "a place whose pastry shops were the finest under heaven". *Listening to A Hundred Tunes while Enjoying the View of Jiangnan* talks of Huaiyang snacks, "Huaiyang snacks and refreshments are known for a perfect combination of freshness and mild sweetness, integration of fish, meat and vegetables, a perfect balance of fluffiness and pliability, and a good marriage of crispness and softness. The most famous are steamed buns called Yang Rong San Mian, a kind of traditional nutritious pastry of Yangzhou, its dual function being beautifying the skin of its customers and enhancing their health and well-being. They are widely appreciated for their small and exquisite shape, wonderful flavors and long-lasting fragrances." Huaiyang snacks in Yangzhou won high praise from gourmets both at home and abroad.

Among the famous master chefs making Huaiyang snacks and desserts during the middle of the Qing Dynasty, the most celebrated was Beauty Shaw in Yizheng county. The pastries she made were said to be as valuable as gold. Yuan Mei, a famous Qing-dynasty writer and gourmet, depicted the beautiful pastry chef in his book *The Menu of Sui Garden*: "Outside the south gate of Yizheng county lives Beauty Shaw, who is an expert in making snacks and desserts. Steamed buns or other pastries made by her are all small, cute and as white as snow." Beauty Shaw is also regarded as one of the top ten master chefs of ancient China by the contemporary Chinese catering circle. Yin Changshan, Zhang Guangqing, Dong De'an, Chen Ende and many others are reputed as modern master chefs of Yangzhou pastry. Take Chen Ende for example. While inheriting the traditional cooking methods, he combined his innovative ideas with classic cooking techniques and recreated the delicate snacks in the Red

开拓创新，开发了以《红楼梦》为题材和背景的“红楼点心”，如银丝挂面、松子鹅油卷、牡丹花样小果、如意锁片、太君酥、蟹黄小饺儿等。

这些大师们先后数次赴国外表演与交流，宣传和弘扬淮扬面点，在他们的努力和带领下，淮扬面点正以前所未有的速度和魅力走向世界，富春茶社的面点便是其中的杰出代表。

富春茶社创建于1885年，它原本是一座栽培四季花卉、制作盆景的花局，后来在花局里办茶社，因经营有方，日益兴盛，成为名闻遐迩的扬州老字号企业。富春茶社以花、茶、点、菜结合，色、香、味、形俱佳，闲、静、雅、适兼优的独特风格和特色，受到社会的好评。富春的“魁龙珠”茶，独家创制，它用魁针、龙井、珠兰三种茶配制而成，色、香、味俱全。富春的众多点心和小吃被评为“中华名小吃”和“中国名点”。三丁包和蟹黄包曾荣获“国家金鼎奖”。千层油糕和翡翠烧卖被称为“扬州双绝”。

·三丁包

·梅兰竹菊酥

·千层油糕

·翡翠烧卖

·枇杷酥

·麻花酥

·菊花包子

·鸡丝卷子

Mansion Banquet style, which is designed to present the theme and background of *A Dream of the Red Mansions*. Some of the delicate snacks are Silver Needle Noodles, Pinenut and Goose-fat Rolls, Flour Fruits in Peony Designs, Rice-flour Pudding, Crisp Cakes and Fried Dumplings Stuffed With Crab-meat. These master chefs have been abroad many times to show their skills in making Huaiyang pastry snacks and share their cooking skills, advocating and developing Huaiyang-style pastry. With their efforts and guidance, Huaiyang pastry industry has become popular at an unprecedented speed and is displaying its radiant charm to the world. The pastry of Fuchun Teahouse is the most outstanding representative of authentic Huaiyang pastries.

Fuchun Teahouse was established in Yangzhou in 1885. It was originally a flora store, which held theme flower fairs according to the season and sold bonsais as well. Later it was converted into a tea house. After painstaking efforts and proper management, Fuchun Teahouse has become a famous Chinese restaurant known for its long history and high quality. As a representative of Yangzhou tea pastry, Fuchun Teahouse has been enjoying a nationwide reputation due to its remarkable combination of flowers, tea, pastries and dishes, whose color, aroma, taste and form are well-balanced as well as its elegant and comfortable environment. Fuchun Teahouse is also famous for its self-made tea Kuilongzhu. Kuizhen from Anhui, Longjing from Zhejiang and Zhulan planted by Fuchun, are the main ingredients of Kuilongzhu, which is a good marriage of Kuizhen's color, Longjing's taste, and Zhulan's flavor. Many dishes, snacks and refreshments from Fuchun Teahouse have been awarded the titles Famous Chinese Snacks and Famous Chinese Refreshments. Dumplings with Juicy Crab Meat Filling and Three-dice Buns once won the Jinding Award (Golden Tripod Award). Thousand Layer Cakes and Steamed Pork and Rice Wraps have been reputed as the Double Wonders of Yanzhou.

第六章
工艺品鉴

扬州工艺美术素以历史悠久、品种丰富、技艺精湛、地方特色鲜明著称于世，2010年扬州被中国工艺美术协会授予“中国传统工艺美术特色基地”的称号。在江苏省政府保护的45个传统工艺品种中，扬州共有玉器、漆器、仿古青铜器、金银制品、刺绣、绒花、绢花、通草花、灯彩、剪纸、瓷刻、竹刻、苏裱、毛笔和红木雕刻共15个品种入选，占全省的三分之一。其中，玉器、漆器、剪纸被列为国家“非物质文化遗产”。另外，扬州的雕版印刷、剪纸已被列入世界“人类非物质文化遗产名录”。

·扬州工艺坊一角

为弘扬传统工艺文化，促进传统工艺技术的发展，扬州在古城区盐阜东路护城河北岸、个园的对面兴建了扬州工艺坊与工艺美术新馆，它是集研发、生产、加工、批发、零售、展示和旅游观光、娱乐休闲、消费购物为一体的综合性工艺美术品市场。

Chapter VI
Craftwork Appreciation

Yangzhou arts and crafts are famous for their long history, exquisite craftsmanship and distinctive local characteristics. China Arts and Crafts Association awarded Yangzhou the title of The Base of Traditional Chinese Arts and Crafts in 2010. There are forty-five traditional arts and crafts under the protection of Jiangsu Province, fifteen of which are from Yangzhou. They are jadeware, lacquerware, pseudo-antique bronze wares, gold and silver ornaments, embroidery, velvet flowers, silk flowers, rice paper flowers, festive lanterns, paper-cutting, porcelain engravings, bamboo engravings, Su mountings, calligraphy brushes and redwood carvings. Among these, jadeware, lacquerware and paper-cutting have been listed as the National Intangible Cultural Heritage, while Yangzhou block printing and paper-cutting have been listed in the World Intangible Cultural Heritage of Humanity.

To better promote the traditional craft culture and to further develop the traditional technology, Yangzhou Craft Workshops and Yangzhou New Art Museum have been established in the old town of Yangzhou, at the Yanfu East Road, north bank of the moat river and just opposite Ge Garden. It is an integrated arts and crafts market, a research and development center, a tourist attraction, as well as a center for the production, processing and sale of Yangzhou handicrafts.

第一节　扬州玉器

扬州是我国玉器的重要产地之一，琢玉工艺源远流长，“天下玉，扬州工”的美誉在玉器行业及收藏界内人人皆知。几千年来，扬州的玉雕师呕心沥血，创制了数量众多、形式各异、巧夺天工的玉器珍宝。

发展历史

早在4000年前的夏代，扬州地区就有玉石琢磨的活动，古籍《书经•禹贡篇》中有“扬州贡瑶琨”的记述。

随着经济和政治的发展，汉代扬州的琢玉工艺，也有了新的进展。从出土的玉器中，可知扬州玉器由小件发展到中件，从一般的装饰品玉镯、玉环发展至观赏的玉蝶、玉璧、辟邪等数十个品种。

唐代的扬州经济繁荣，百业兴旺，玉文化有了新的发展。一方面，贵族豪门常用玉件装饰楼阁，即所谓“雕栏玉户”；另一方面，民间以小件玉器作为佩饰用品也开始流行。另外，扬州玉器和琢玉技艺也陆续对外交流，如鉴真东渡日本传教，就带有玉工、画师等人。

宋、元、明时代，扬州玉器向陈列品方面发展，花鸟、炉瓶等品种日见丰富，造型、琢磨艺术水平大为提高。琢玉中的镂空、圆雕技法始于宋代。元代，扬州艺人已经开始用天然玉石为材料，制作“山子雕”。明代，扬州玉器开始形成典雅秀丽的风格。

Section One Yangzhou Jadeware

Yangzhou is one of the most famous areas in China for its jade production and long history in jade carving. The saying that "Yangzhou jade carvings are known for their delicate, graceful and exquisite style" is well-known in the jade industry as well as the jade collection circle. Over thousands of years, generations of jade craftsmen have devoted themselves to continuing and innovating the ancient traditional skills to create many exquisite jade articles of various shapes and sizes.

History

The craft of Yangzhou jade carving originated from as early as 4,000 BC, during the Xia Dynasty and at that time "Yangzhou jade articles were carved as tributes to the kings", which is cited in the Tribute of Yu of *The Book of History.*

Due to economic and political development, Yangzhou jade carving was further advanced during the Han Dynasty. Many varieties of excavated jade relics in Yangzhou displayed the developmental course of jade carving craft over time, from small to middle size, from ornamental jade bracelets and rings to the more exquisite jade butterflies, small wheel jade and talismanic jade ornaments.

The economic prosperity of the Tang Dynasty led to a new development in Yangzhou jade carving industry. At that time, wealthy and noble familie usually had their homes ornamented with jade objects, sparking the phrase "carved pillars and jade houses". On the other hand, the ordinary people began wearing small jade ornaments. Meanwhile, Yangzhou jade items and the jade carving craft spread all over China. The Master Jian Zhen of the Tang Dynasty crossed the ocean eastward to Japan to preach Buddhism, bringing jade craftsmen and painters with him.

During the Song, Yuan and Ming Dynasties, Yangzhou jade carving branched out in making exhibits. The jade market was rich in jade articles such as birds, flowers, incense vases and Yangzhou jade shaping and polishing skills reached new heights. Hollowing and circular engraving techniques in jade carving date back to the Song Dynasty. In the Yuan Dynasty, Yangzhou jade craftsmen began to create Shanzidiao (rockery sculpture) out of natural jade stones. By the Ming Dynasty, the elegant and beautiful style of Yangzhou jade carvings came into being.

·普渡众生

清代，扬州玉器品种齐全，琢玉艺术水平空前提高，在乾隆年间达到全盛。扬州成为全国玉材的主要集散地和玉器生产制作中心之一，每年要向朝廷进贡大量玉器。目前，保存在北京故宫博物院中轻则千斤、重达万斤的近十件大玉山，多半为扬州琢制。当时，扬州玉器“南秀北雄”的艺术风格初步显现，大型玉器表现为庄重、质朴、浑厚的特色，而中小件玉器则典雅秀丽。

20世纪50年代，扬州琢玉业开始复兴，成为中国现代玉器的主要产区，在全国同行业中名列前茅，多次荣获国家级奖项。现在，扬州有顾永骏、薛春梅、江春源、高毅进等中国工艺美术大师，在他们的引领下，扬州玉器精品迭出，优秀作品层出不穷，在国内外享有盛誉。

工艺特点

扬州玉雕创造性地将阴线刻、深浅浮雕、立体圆雕、镂空雕、环链工艺等多种技法融于一体，形成了“浑厚、圆润、儒雅、灵秀、精巧”的基本特征，以其独有的艺术魅力著称于世。

·荷花仙子

扬州玉雕，首先是将绘画艺术同琢制工艺相结合，准确地反映画面内容及情节。许多玉雕的艺术主题都是以名画或诗为蓝本，再根据玉料的颜色、大小，进行再创作，充分利用玉料的立体形象，将平面画展示的内容琢成一幅具有透视效果的立体画。其次，在场景雕造上，善于运用高浮雕和圆雕的手法，表现远近、高低、上下不同层次的景物。大型玉雕的玉质中，常含有许多颜色不同的杂质和较重的纹理，但玉工能够充分发挥想象力，将其琢成嶙峋的怪石、枯黄的树叶、崎岖的山道等，与画面内容紧密相联，情景交融，形成强烈的艺术感染力。

In the Qing Dynasty, Yangzhou jade articles were of great varieties and the jade craft reached its peak especially during the reign of Emperor Qianlong. Then, Yangzhou was the country's main distributing center of jade materials and one of the important jade production centers. Yangzhou had to send a yearly tribute of jade articles to the imperial court. At present, about ten large jadewares are preserved in the Palace Museum in Beijing. The lightest of them weighs about 500 kg, some even weighing up to 5,000 kg. More than half of them were made in Yangzhou. At that time, the artistic style of "integrating the northern grandness with the southern fineness" of Yangzhou jadewares made its first appearance. Large jadewares characterized solemnity, simplicity and strength, while small and medium-sized pieces were dainty and elegant.

After the 1950s, Yangzhou jade carving revived. The city once more became the main production center of modern jade products in China, and Yangzhou jade stays in ahead in the jade industry and has won many national awards. Now, there are some famous Chinese artists living in Yangzhou, such as Gu Yongjun, Xue Chunmei, Jiang Chunyuan and Gao Yijin. With their guidance, fine quality Yangzhou jadewares are being produced, enjoying high reputation both at home and abroad.

Features

Yangzhou jade carving craft creatively integrates various sculpting techniques which make the jade look simple, vigorous, smooth, elegant and delicate, thereby gaining world fame for their unique artistic charm.

Yangzhou jade carving combines painting techniques with those of carving, accurately depicting the content and plot of a scene. The themes and subjects of many jade carvings are based on some famous paintings and poems. Skilled craftsmen design their pieces according to the colors and size of the stone, make full use of the stereoscopic features of jade carvings and turn the content of a plane surface painting into a vivid scene with real depth and perspective. Techniques adopted in scene carving are mainly high-relief carving and circular carving, through which jade carving can fully present the close-up and the background scenery with varying heights and levels. The raw jade used for large pieces of jadeware is usually a coarse-grained jade with many impurities of different colors. The jade craftsmen in Yangzhou can expressively bring out the beauty of the raw jade and truly depict the content of the painting by making the raw jade into jadewares such as jagged rocks, withered and yellow leaves and rugged mountain passes.

扬州玉雕尤以山子雕独具一格。山子雕是一种起源于明代、盛行于清代的中国传统玉雕形式，主要是在外形呈不规则的卵形籽玉上，或在各种山石形状的石料上，经过精心构思，以各种人物和诗词典故为内容，构思山水、花草树木、鸟禽走兽，用圆雕、浮雕、镂空雕的方式制作成立体画面。这种形式的玉雕作品，造型浑圆典雅，给人们带来赏心悦目的视觉效果和美的享受。

玉器珍品

扬州玉器分炉瓶、人物、花鸟、走兽、仿古、山子雕六个类别，使用的玉料品种齐全，花色繁多，有新疆的白玉、青玉、碧玉，辽宁的岫玉、玛瑙、黄玉，江苏的水晶，湖北的绿苗、松耳石，广东的南方玉及巴西的玉石，缅甸的翡翠，阿富汗的青金，加拿大的碧玉和日本的珊瑚等。

《大禹治水图》玉山，高224厘米，宽96厘米，底座高60厘米，重达5300公斤，为世界和田玉玉器之王。玉山是在清乾隆年间，根据宋代绘画《大禹治水图》，采用新疆青白二色和田玉雕琢而成，现藏于北京故宫博物院。玉山雕琢崇山峻岭、飞瀑流泉、古木苍松，气势磅礴，人物山水风景如画，堪称稀世珍品。

《秋山行旅图》玉山，高130厘米，最宽处74厘米，最厚处20厘米，重1000多斤，现珍藏于北京故宫博物院。这件玉山制作于清乾隆年间，玉料产自和田，玉质洁白，中间杂有淡黄色斑。玉石上的崇山峻岭、苍松翠柏、山

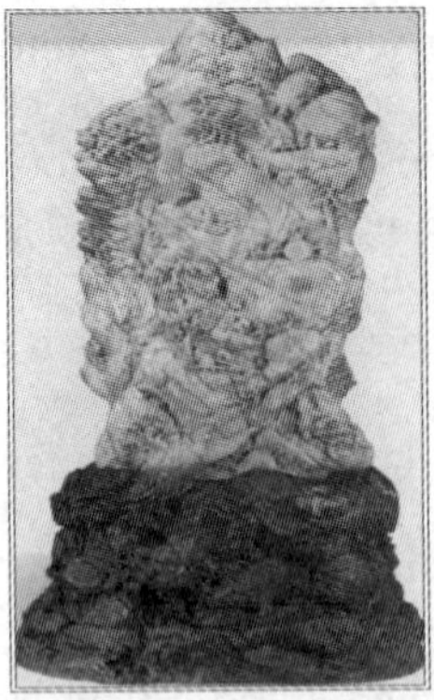

· 大禹治水图

· 秋山行旅图

The Shanzidiao technique is quite unique, demonstrating the exquisite craftsmanship of Yangzhou jade carving. It was a traditional carving skill which originated from the Ming Dynasty and prevailed in the Qing Dynasty. Pebble nephrite with irregular shapes and various mountain-like stones are generally used, and the techniques of circular carving, relief carving and sculpture are employed in this technique. Thus, three-dimensional Yangzhou jade articles are created to vividly depict various characters, poems and literary quotations. The objects include landscape, images of flowers, plants and trees and also the figures of birds and various animals. This kind of jade carving is perfectly round and elegant in shape, giving people visual satisfaction.

Jade Treasures

Yangzhou jade articles fall into six categories: incense vases, human figures, flowers and birds, animals, pseudo-antique jade carvings and Shanzidiao. Raw materials for Yangzhou jade carving are diverse in category and rich in color, including white jade, gray jade and jasper from Xinjiang Uygur Autonomous Region, Xiuyan jade, agate and topaz from Liaoning Province, crystal from Jiangsu Province, malachite and turquoise from Hubei Province, Xinyi jade from Guangdong Province, as well as jade from Brazil, jadeite from Myanmar, lapis lazuli from Afghanistan, jasper from Canada and coral from Japan.

The jade sculpture Sage King Yu Controlling the Floods is a jade rarity with a height of 224 cm, a width of 96 cm and a 60-centimeter-high pedestal, weighing 5,300kg, making it the largest Hetian jade in the world. This magnificent Qing-dynasty jade sculpture is based on a famous Song Dynasty painting Sage King Yu Controlling the Floods. This large piece of jadeware was made of white and gray jade from Xinjiang during the Emperor Qianlong's reign. It is now preserved in the Palace Museum in Beijing. This masterpiece of jade sculpture portrays the full beauty of a grand, magnificent and picturesque scene with high mountains, cascading waterfalls, flowing springs, ancient trees, green pines and lifelike characters.

The jade sculpture Traveling amid Mountains in Autumn is also kept in the Palace Museum in Beijing. It weighs over 500 kg and measures 130 cm high, 74 cm wide at its widest and 20 cm thick at its thickest. It is made of pure white jade mingled with some primrose yellow dapples from Xinjiang during the reign of Emperor Qianlong in the Qing Dynasty. The jade sculpture depicts a beautiful mountain

间茅舍栩栩如生，崎岖山路上几个行路人正赶着驮队向山上进发，呈现出一派深秋山林景象。

1986年琢成的《白玉五行塔》，中央主塔七层八角形，高105厘米，宽32厘米，四周有四座六角形的分塔，以8根玉链从四方连接分塔，构成群体，塔群东南西北的四个正面各有两尊玉坐狮，玉狮之间又有一座玉制香炉，主塔和分塔之间，地面上又有走廊相接。这件玉器充分展示了精细的镂雕工艺，曾获得“国家珍品金杯奖”，现珍藏于中国工艺美术馆。

1986年琢成的《聚珍图》碧玉山，高120厘米，宽90厘米，重达1000多

· 白玉五行塔

· 聚珍图

公斤，以著名石刻为题材，集乐山大佛、大足石佛、龙门大佛和云冈石佛于一体，构成深邃幽秘的福地仙境。作品由顾永骏设计，其构思之巧、造型之妙、工艺之精、手法之奇达到了出神入化的境界，成为山子雕的代表作。作品获“国家珍品金杯奖”，被中国工艺美术馆作为收藏。

2004年琢成的《螳螂白菜》获中国工艺美术精品博览会特等奖。作品由江春源设计、时春梅制作，以缅甸翡翠为原料，长90厘米，宽与高各56厘米，净重达150多公斤，菜帮层叠紧裹，菜叶蓬松舒卷，菜根屈曲缠绕，两只凌空镂雕的螳螂栖息于白菜之上，惟妙惟肖，活灵活现，散发出温馨而恬然的田园神韵。在上海世博会期间，本作品曾作为江苏馆的“镇馆之宝”向中外参观者展示。

· 螳螂白菜

sight in late autumn with lofty mountains, ancient trees, green pines, huts in mountain and the rough mountain roads where some travelers on horsebacks are heading for the mountains.

The White Jade Five Elements Tower was completed in 1986. The main tower has seven layers and eight sides and measures 105 cm long by 32 cm wide, with 8 main jade chains linking the four towers in four directions to form the complex. On each of the four sides of the complex sit two jade lions, with a jade incense burner between them. The main tower and the other four towers are separated, but linked to each other by the ground corridors. This jadeware fully demonstrates the exquisite craftsmanship of Yangzhou jade carving. It was awarded the National Golden Cup Award and is kept in the National Museum of Arts and Crafts.

The jasper sculpture Fantastic Get-together of Buddhas, which is a recreation of the subject from a famous stone sculpture, was completed in 1986. It measures 120 cm high by 32 cm wide and weighs over 1,000 kg. Giant Buddha from Leshan, Stone Buddha from Dazu, Giant Buddha from Longmen and Stone Buddha from Yungang are having a happy get-together on this jasper sculpture, making it a deep and serene fairyland. This jade sculpture was designed by Gu Yongjun, who employed excellent techniques to create this exquisite composition. His skilled techniques and mastery of utilizing jade shapes make this jasper sculpture a masterpiece of Shanzidiao. It was awarded the National Golden Cup Award and is currently kept in the National Museum of Arts and Crafts.

The emerald sculpture Mantis and Chinese Cabbage was awarded the Special Prize in the 2004 China Arts and Crafts Boutique Expo. The jade cabbage, designed by Jiang Chunyuan, was carved by Shi Chunmei out of a single piece of high quality jadeite from Myanmar. It is 90 cm in length, 56 cm in height and width. The 150 kg white jade piece seems to float within a light purple hue. Thanks to the fine craftsmanship, the white stem and outer leaves of the cabbage are vividly carved, and on the naturally curling light-green tender leaves, two lifelike mantises are resting. In the 2010 Shanghai World Expo, as the Treasure of Jiangsu Pavilion, Mantis and Chinese Cabbage was shown to visitors from home and abroad.

中国玉器博物馆

2010年，原扬州玉器博物馆提升为中国玉器博物馆，这标志着我国首家“国字号”玉器博物馆落户扬州。中国玉器博物馆与扬州玉器厂生产基地东西相对，建筑面积2875平方米，分为“扬州古代玉器”、“扬州玉器工艺”、“现代扬州玉器”三个展区，采用彩色雕塑模型、沙盘、古玉、现代玉器精品、玉石材料及仿古件等实物、图片的形式，展示丰富多彩的扬州玉器文化。

中国玉器博物馆作为历史传承的载体，将有效地保护扬州玉雕这项国家“非物质文化遗产”，弘扬中华玉文化，为推动中国传统工艺美术事业发展发挥重要作用。

· 中国玉器博物馆

China Jade Museum

In 2010, China opened its first national-level jade museum, which was updated from the original Yangzhou Jadeware Museum, in picturesque Yangzhou. China Jade Museum is opposite Yangzhou Jadeware Factory and covers an area of 2,875 square meters. It consists of three exhibition areas: Yangzhou Ancient Jade Relics, Crafts of Jade Carving and Modern Jade Masterpieces. Yangzhou jade culture is fully displayed in photographs, color sculpture models, sand tables, ancient jade articles, modern jade masterpieces, raw jade materials and pseudo-antique jade articles.

As one of the carriers of history, China Jade Museum will play a prominent role in effectively protecting Yangzhou jade carving—the National Intangible Cultural Heritage, and in further advancing and enriching China's jade culture and promoting the prosperity and development of traditional arts and crafts.

第二节　扬州漆器

漆器是利用天然漆，运用雕刻、彩绘等多种工艺手段制作而成的精美器具。扬州是全国漆器的重点产区，品种齐全，技艺精湛，风格独特，扬州漆器是我国传统文化艺术宝库中的一颗璀璨明珠。2006年，扬州漆器被列为国家“非物质文化遗产”。

发展历史

扬州漆器起源于战国，兴旺于秦汉，鼎盛于明清，发展于现代，有约2400年的悠久历史。

据史书记载，扬州漆器早在战国时期就达到了一定的生产规模和较高的制作工艺水平。国家博物馆收藏了大量战国时期扬州的漆器。右图是出土的战国时期彩绘漆涡纹方耳杯，色彩鲜艳，画面清晰，是当时的一种饮食器皿。

· 战国彩绘漆涡纹方耳杯

汉代，扬州漆器生产不仅规模大、范围广、品种多，而且技艺精湛、水平高超。从上世纪50年代以来，在扬州郊区许多汉代墓葬中出土的漆器及其残片多达万件。器物中有饮食、梳妆、文房、器械、丧葬等用具，体现了漆器广泛的用途。其装饰工艺则有彩绘、针刻、贴金、金银嵌等类别，其胎骨以木制为最多，说明扬州为我国木胎漆器的发源地。

· 汉代彩绘云气纹漆卮

唐代，扬州漆器既是贡品，也是出口商品中的抢手货。当时扬州经济繁荣，手工业相当发达，彩绘、雕漆和金银脱等漆器制作愈益精细，螺钿镶嵌

Section Two Yangzhou Lacquerware

Lacquer work is an ancient technique that uses the sap of the lacquer tree. Craftsmen process the sap for use in delicate lacquerware with engravings, color designs, etc. Yangzhou is an important area in China for producing exquisite lacquerware in great varieties and special styles. Yangzhou lacquerware was listed as a National Intangible Cultural Heritage in 2006 and is a shinning pearl in the traditional Chinese culture and art treasures.

History

Yangzhou lacquerware has a history of about 2,400 years and continues to develop in modern times. Yangzhou lacquerware originated in the Warring States Period, flourished in the Qin and Han Dynasties, and reached its peak in the Ming and Qing Dynasties.

As early as in the Warring States Period, Yangzhou lacquerware showed good manufacturing skills, with relatively large-scale production, as documented by historical records. The National Museum of China preserves a large quantity of Yangzhou lacquerware. On the right is an ear-shaped lacquer cup with color painting from the Warring States Period. It is a vessel for holding food and drinks with light colors and clear painting.

By the Han Dynasty, Yangzhou lacquer technology and craftsmanship had reached a fairly high level, and the production scale and the varieties had greatly increased. Yangzhou lacquerware was used in every sphere of society for many purposes. For example, since the 1950s, in the Yangzhou suburbs, up to 10,000 pieces of lacquerware and fragments were unearthed, including daily utensils, dressing sets, utensils of the study, weapons and tomb ware. By then Yangzhou lacquerware had already become a developed art form. Color painting, carving, gilt and inlaid gold and silver patterns appeared on the lacquerware at that time. The unearthed artifacts show that the making of Yangzhou lacquerware usually had a wooden body, which proves that Yangzhou is the cradle of wooden lacquerware.

In the Tang Dynasty, Yangzhou lacquerware became such a cherished product that it was very popular as a gift of tribute and for export. At that time, Yangzhou enjoyed great economic and artistic prosperity. Owing to the application of such lacquer techniques as color

工艺亦具有很高水平。鉴真东渡日本时，携带了几十件漆盒、漆盘。日本奈良唐招提寺的鉴真大师宝像，就是唐代漆器工艺中的夹紵胎塑像，它由鉴真大师的弟子制作，现在是日本的国宝。

·日本唐招提寺的鉴真大师像

宋、元两代，扬州漆器在继承传统的基础上有了新的发展。雕漆工艺水平明显提高，还出现了“软螺钿”这一新的镶嵌工艺品种，这使得漆器的品种更加丰富多样。

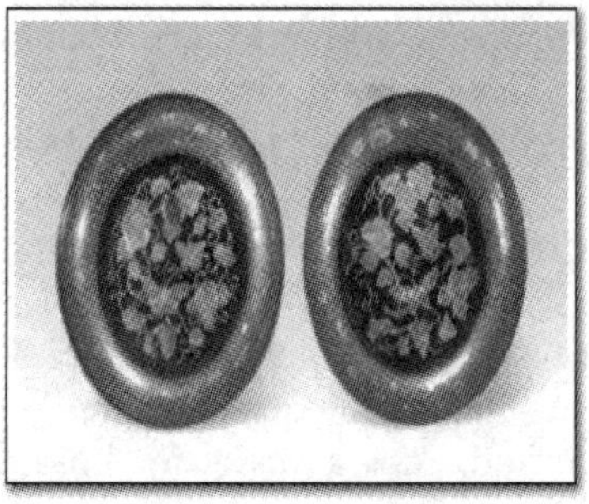

·宋代软螺钿瓜碟盘

明清时期，扬州漆器发展至顶峰，成为全国漆器制作中心，除了彩绘和雕漆外，平磨螺钿、骨石镶嵌、百宝镶嵌等新工艺得到普遍应用。明代，还兴起了点螺漆器，万历年间的漆艺大师江千里就以制作点螺漆器著称于世。至清代后期，扬州漆器远销南洋及欧美等国，年销量达两万多件。清代出现了一批著名的漆艺大师，如卢映之、王国琛等人，他们将雕漆和百宝镶嵌工艺相结合，创制了“雕漆嵌玉”这一扬州独有的地方工艺。卢映之还恢复了失传已久的漆砂砚制作工艺。

抗日战争爆发后，漆器生产萧条，生产作坊相继歇业，一些作坊被日寇烧光，剩下的也只是勉强维持生产，扬州漆器处于人亡艺绝的边缘。

新中国建立后，在党和政府的高度重视和亲切关怀下，扬州传统漆器工艺不仅得到恢复，而且经过多年的努力，扬州已经发展成为全国漆器行业中规模最大、品种最多、技术力量最为雄厚的重点产区。其中，值得一提的是，扬州漆器厂的张宇、赵如柏、池家俊三位中国工艺美术大师，为漆器传统工艺的继承和发扬做出了巨大的贡献。

painting, lacquer engraving and the inlaid gold and silver lacquer, lacquer works were becoming more and more elaborate. Meanwhile, the technique of mother-of-pearl inlays reached its maturity. On his journey to Japan, the master Jian Zhen brought along with him dozens of lacquer boxes and platters. One example of the ramie cloth lacquer works in the Tang Dynasty is the statue of Jian Zhen in Toshodai-ji, a national treasure of Japan, made in dry lacquer by Jian Zhen's students after his parinirvana.

In the Song and Yuan Dynasties, many new techniques and decorative methods were developed from the traditional lacquerware techniques. Yangzhou lacquerware boasted a full range of varieties, with the improvement of lacquer engraving and the emergence of soft mother-of-pearl inlaying.

Yangzhou lacquerware reached its heyday by the Ming and Qing Dynasties when Yangzhou was the national center of lacquerware production. Many new techniques and designs involving mother-of-pearl polishing, bone inlaying and hundred-treasure inlaying as well as color painting and lacquer engraving were widely applied. There were also the seashell inlays of the Ming Dynasty. A master craftsman, Jiang Qianli, was famous during the reign of Emperor Wanli for making lacquerware with seashell inlays. In the late Qing Dynasty, Yangzhou lacquerware products were exported to Southeast Asia, Europe and America, with an annual sale of more than 20,000 pieces. The Qing Dynasty also saw a large number of master craftsmen like Lu Yingzhi and Wang Guochen, who integrated lacquer engraving and hundred-treasure inlaying, creating a unique Yangzhou lacquerware technique—engraving with jade inlaying. Lu Yingzhi also reinvented the long lost sand-lacquer inkstone craft.

After the breakout of the War of Resistance against Japan, the lacquerware production fell dramatically. Most workshops closed and some were even burned to ashes by the Japanese invaders. Those left could barely survive. Yangzhou lacquerware handicraft was on the point of extinction.

Since the founding of the People's Republic of China, the Communist Party of China and the Chinese government have given high priority to the restoration of Yangzhou lacquerware craftsmanship. After years of effort, Yangzhou has developed and re-established itself as a main center for lacquerware industry, with the largest-scale production, the most varieties and the strongest technical force. It is worth mentioning that three Masters of Arts and Crafts in China, Zhang Yu, Zhao Rubai and Chi Jiajun from Yangzhou Lacquerware Factory, have made great contributions to the development and preservation of the traditional Yangzhou lacquerware craft.

· 明代缠织莲纹填漆盒

· 清代描金花卉纹黑漆盘

工艺特点

目前，扬州漆器装饰工艺有刻漆、雕漆、雕漆嵌玉、骨石镶嵌、点螺、平磨螺钿、漆砂砚、彩绘、雕填、撒螺屑等十大类。下面介绍几种主要类型：

刻漆是先在制作好的漆坯件上，运用各种刀具刻出各类图案，然后根据画面要求进行填色、贴金、撒螺屑等，工艺流程可归纳为刻、铲、批、作、贴、撒六步。

雕漆工艺创制于唐代，该工艺须先在所制器物上涂数十层到几百层中国大漆，然后雕刻各种图案和锦纹。到了明清时期，扬州漆器艺人在雕漆工艺基础上，选用翡翠、玛瑙、青石、白玉、珊瑚、碧玉、珠贝、象牙等几十种高档材料，雕琢成各种浮雕图案镶嵌在雕漆锦纹之上，成为扬州独特的雕漆嵌玉工艺。

平磨螺钿工艺具有浓厚的地方风格，是选用优质的珍珠贝、云母、石决明等材料，经打磨成不同色彩的薄片，根据画面需求切拉成各种块面，平嵌在各类器物漆坯上，经过精致髹漆工艺，使产品具有光亮如镜、黑白分明、高雅素洁的艺术效果。

点螺工艺为国家重点保护的高档工艺，选用自然色彩的夜光螺、珍珠贝、石决明等高档材料精制成薄如蝉翼、小如针尖、细若秋毫的螺片，用特制的工具一点一丝地点填在平整光滑的漆坯上，经过精致的髹漆工艺，使产品具有色彩绚丽、随光变幻的艺术风格。

Features

Now Yangzhou lacquerware decoration techniques can be classified into ten categories, including lacquer engraving, lacquer carving, engraving with jade inlaying, bone-and-stone inlaying, mother-of-pearl dotting, mother-of-pearl polishing, sand-lacquer inkstone making, color painting, carving and filling-in and mother-of-pearl spraying. We will have a look at some main categories.

Lacquer engraving involves applying thick layers of lacquer on a wooden core, carving out exquisite patterns on the surface, filling in different colors and dusting the lacquered surface with gold or fine shell powder. The overall process can be divided into six steps: engraving, cutting, coating, coloring, sticking and spraying.

Lacquer carving was created during the Tang Dynasty. The first step is to coat dozens of or even several hundred layers of the Chinese raw lacquer on an object and then to carve various patterns and designs with a knife. During the Ming and Qing Dynasties, on the basis of lacquer carving, the craftsmen of Yangzhou lacquerware selected and used jadeite, agate, lapis, white jade, coral, green jade, pearl shells, ivory and other valuable materials to carve different relief designs and then inlaid them onto the lacquer carving decorative patterns. This creative combination of lacquer carving and jewel inlaying is unique to Yangzhou.

Yangzhou mother-of-pearl polishing bears a strong stamp of local style. The process begins with selecting the materials: oriental pearl shells, isinglass or abalone. The materials are meticulously polished into thin colored pieces, which are cut into different sizes. The pieces are then inlaid onto the object being crafted. A fine coating of lacquer together with polishing produces plain and elegant lacquer works which are characterized by bright luster with sharp contrasts between light and dark areas.

The mother-of-pearl dotting is protected by the Chinese government as a highly confidential technique. The process of this technique is to select green snails, pearl shells, abalone and other valuable materials and to cut them into pieces as thin as cicadas' wings, as small as pinpoint and as dainty as tiny hair. The materials are then dotted onto the smooth surface of the lacquerware with special tools one by one, using delicate lacquer-coating techniques. The products have gorgeous colors and can change with light.

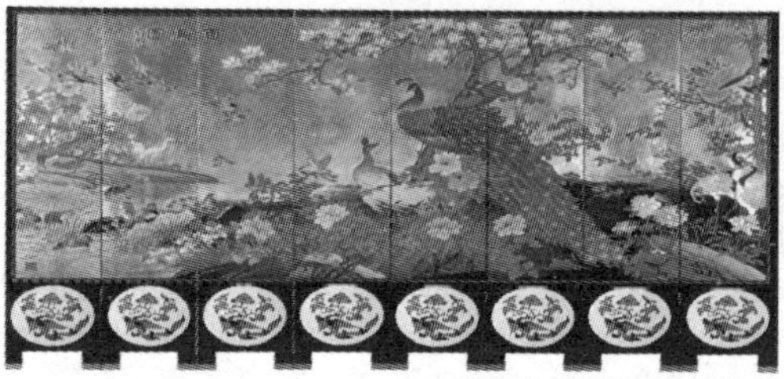

·刻漆贴金《百鸟图》屏风

漆砂砚工艺在清后期失传，1979年至1981年扬州漆器厂研制恢复。它以金丝楠木为胎，砚身用整木雕制，砚盒则用点螺工艺，砚池采用高岭土、细粒金刚砂和中国大漆精心配制而成，具有结构紧密、耐研磨、不伤笔毫、发墨快、不吸水等优良性能。1985年，彭真委员长访问日本时，将漆砂砚《醉翁亭》作为国礼赠送给日本天皇。

·点螺《凤戏牡丹》台屏

·漆砂砚《醉翁亭》

漆器珍品

《和平颂》、《喜上梅梢》特大挂屏，是由著名画家、教育家陈之佛和姜壁设计，由扬州市著名工艺大师梁国海等人于1959年精心制作的雕漆嵌玉珍品，曾陈列在北京人民大会堂江苏厅二十多年。这两件精品采用了珊瑚、翡翠、玛瑙、稀有黑墨玉等数种名贵高档玉料雕琢成花鸟图案，镶嵌在涂有百余层漆的雕漆锦纹版面上，花鸟形象栩栩如生、生动优美，使人感到一片盎然春意。

《松龄鹤寿》三折屏是由池家俊创作的雕漆嵌玉珍品。漆屏上郁郁青松迎向喷薄而出的红日，牡丹、梅花、水仙、灵芝盛开着，八只用白玉、玛瑙、珊瑚等材料精心雕琢成的丹顶鹤，或在潺潺溪流间引亢高歌，或在祥云间振翅飞翔，背面彩绘寿星，寓示着多福多寿的意境。本作品共制作了三幅，其中一幅在1983年作为国礼赠送给了日本天皇。

After several years of research and experimentation (1979—1981), Yangzhou Lacquerware Factory succeeded in reinventing the sand-lacquer inkstone technique, which was lost in the late Qing Dynasty. Using golden Nanmu carved from a single log, the sand-lacquer inkstone has its reservoir painted with lacquer that is mixed with sand particles to facilitate the grinding of ink. Thus, the sand-lacquer inkstone is refined, nonporous, incredibly durable and capable of making good, dark ink easily but without damaging the hairs of the brush, which makes for an excellent inkstone. On his official visit to Japan in 1985, Peng Zhen, Chairman of the NPC Standing Committee, presented the Japanese Emperor with the Sand-lacquer Inkstone of Drunken Man's Pavilion as a national gift.

Lacquerware Treasures

An Ode to Peace and the Cheerful Magpies on Blossoming Plum Trees, two large-size hanging panels, were designed by the renowned painter and educator Chen Zhifo and Jiang Bi and made by Liang Guohai, a well-known craftsman in Yangzhou, and his colleagues in 1959. These two works were exquisitely carved and inlaid with jewels. For over two decades they were hung in Jiangsu Chamber of the Great Hall of the People. The making of the two works involved carving decorative birds and floral designs out of high-grade jewels like fine coral, jade, agate, and rare black jade. The jewels were inlaid in wooden panels coated with hundreds of layers of lacquer, showing vivid and beautiful images of flowers, birds and spring landscape.

The carved jade-inlaid three-panel screen Age-old Pines and Long-life Cranes was created by Chi Jiajun. The screen depicts a merry scene of happiness and longevity. Green pines are greeting the rising sun. Peonies, plums, narcissi and ganodermas are in full blossom. Eight red-crowned cranes carved out of white jade, agate, coral and other jewels come in different shapes. Some are chirping and singing by a gurgling stream. Some are flapping their wings over auspicious clouds. On the back of the screen is a color painting of Chinese God of Longevity. Three copies of the same design were produced. In 1983, one of them was presented to the Japanese Emperor as a national gift.

· 雕漆嵌玉《松龄鹤寿》

《江山神韵》大地屏是2002年完成的纯雕漆作品。它是由张宇根据北京故宫所藏宋代画作《渔村小雪图》为蓝本，按雕漆工艺的特点进行设计，赵如柏领衔制作而成。画面中山峦起伏、树木葱葱、古建房廊、飞瀑激流，雕刻艺术独具匠心，层次清晰、气势雄伟，让人叹为观止。整幅作品充分体现了扬州雕漆工艺古朴端庄、秀丽精巧、光滑圆润、精细入微的风格特点。

· 雕漆《江山神韵》

The large-size floor screen Romantic Charm of the Landscape completed in 2002 belongs to the class of carved lacquer. Its designer Zhang Yu borrowed the scene from A Fishing Village after a Light Snow, a landscape painting in the Song Dynasty, which is currently kept in the Palace Museum in Beijing. In this design, he abided by the characteristics of lacquer carving. The floor screen was carved by a team headed by the master Zhao Rubai. This ingenious work presents rolling hills, verdant and thick trees, ancient buildings and galleries, flying falls and raging current. It also fully displays the features of Yangzhou lacquerware: simple and elegant, beautiful and exquisite, smooth and mellow, refined and elaborate.

第三节　扬州剪纸

扬州剪纸线条清秀流畅，构图精巧雅致，形象夸张简洁，技法变中求新，为中国南方民间剪纸艺术的代表之一。

起源与发展

扬州剪纸源于隋朝，至今已有2000多年的历史。扬州是中国剪纸流行最早的地区之一。

隋朝，扬州逢年过节即有“剪彩胜”的习俗。传说隋炀帝下扬州时，冬季花木凋谢，便令宫女剪彩锦为花叶，或装点枝条，或飘浮于水塘湖面，以模拟春景夏色。自此，“剪彩胜”在扬州民间就长盛不衰。

唐代，扬州造纸业发达，大量生产高质量的贡纸，从而促进了剪纸艺术的发展。当时，扬州已有剪纸迎春的风俗，有书记载：“立春之日，民间剪纸为花，又剪为春蝶、春钱、春胜，或悬于佳人之首，或缀于花下，相观以为乐。”唐代的剪纸有了迷信色彩，民间剪纸人、纸马、纸钱用于祭奠鬼神。

清代，扬州经济繁荣，市民讲究穿戴，服饰与布织用品都以绣花为美。绣花都要用剪纸为底样，因此以剪纸为生的民间艺人很多，最著名的大师是道光年间的鲍均，在他的剪下，花、鸟、鱼、蝶无不神形兼备，引人入胜，故而被誉为“神剪”。清末以来扬州剪纸艺术的杰出代表有张金盛和张永寿父子。

·清·鲍均·《设色虫草册页》

Section Three Yangzhou Paper-cutting

Yangzhou paper-cutting is known for its clear and fluent lines, fine and elegant patterns, simple and exaggerated images, novel and creative techniques. It represents the paper-cutting styles of Southern China.

Origin and Development

Yangzhou paper-cutting, with a history of over 2,000 years, can be dated back to the Sui Dynasty, making Yangzhou one of the places where paper-cutting first became popular.

In the Sui Dynasty, the people of Yangzhou had the custom of cutting colorful paper or silks and satins to celebrate festivals. According to the legend, during the Sui Dynasty, Emperor Yang came to Yangzhou three times. In winter, the flowers and trees in the garden withered. The Emperor ordered the maids to cut fine silks and satins into flowers and leaves and use them to decorate the trees and ponds, mimicking the looks of spring and summer. Since then, "colorful brocade cutting" has been a popular folk decoration art in Yangzhou.

In the Tang Dynasty, the paper-making industry was highly developed and a large amount of high-quality paper was made as tributes to the Court. This helped promote the development of the paper-cutting art. At that time, the people of Yangzhou practiced the custom of embracing spring with paper cuts, as documented in books: on the day of Spring Beginning, people would cut paper into floral patterns, butterflies, coins and handkerchiefs, used to decorate flowers or worn by ladies. They took delight in appreciating the paper-cuts. In the Tang Dynasty, paper cutting began to take on a superstitious note, as people cut out paper characters, money, horses and other funeral objects as sacrifices to ghosts and gods.

In the Qing Dynasty, due to economic prosperity, the people of Yangzhou became interested in wearing fine clothing, particularly embroidered clothing. The embroidery patterns were based on paper-cuts. Many craftsmen earned their livelihood by the art of paper-cutting. The most well-known of them was Bao Jun, a paper-cutting master, living in the reign of Emperor Daoguang. He won a high reputation as Magic Scissors for his refined cutting skills. His paper-cut flowers, birds, fishes and plates were all lifelike and fascinating, demonstrating a unity of form and spirit. Since the late Qing Dynasty there have been two outstanding Yangzhou master paper-cutters, Zhang Jinsheng and his son Zhang Yongshou.

新中国成立后，剪纸同其他传统手工艺一样得到了党和政府的重视。1955年，成立了民间工艺社（现为扬州工艺厂），把民间的剪纸艺人组织起来，并创造了良好的工作条件，大大激发了他们的创作热情。2007年，中国剪纸博物馆落户于盐商名宅汪氏小苑后花园内，推动了“扬州剪纸”这一文化品牌的发展。

工艺特点

扬州剪纸题材广泛，有人物花卉、鸟兽虫鱼、奇山异景、名胜古迹等，尤以四时花卉见长。扬州剪纸有的以大块面为主调，有的以密密细丝般的线条为主调，有的以挺直刚劲的线条为主调，有的以曲而柔的线条为主调，其特点可概括为“精、秀、灵、雅”四个字，具体表现为：

线条清秀流畅。扬州剪纸多用镂空的技法，阳纹的剪纸线线相连，阴纹的剪纸线线相断，从而产生了千刻不落、万剪不断的线条结构，这是剪纸艺术的一个重要特点。

构图精巧雅致。扬州剪纸讲究造型雅致，依据形象与内容的联系，较多地使用组合的手法，常用二维的手法表现出三维的空间，从而产生图案的形式美。

·李烈峰·《百鹤图》

形象夸张简洁。扬州剪纸在处理形象时，既要抓住物象特征，又要做到线条连接自然，使造型有适度的夸张变形。

技法变中求新。扬州剪纸的许多特点和风格都是由技法的求变求新而产生的。扬州剪纸巧妙运用各种技法，形成了特有的“剪味纸感”。

After the founding of the People's Republic of China, the Communist Party of China and the Chinese government recognized the importance of paper-cutting like many other folk arts and crafts. In 1955, the Agency of Folk Arts and Crafts was established (nowadays Yangzhou Arts and Crafts Factory), where folk artists were organized together and given good working conditions, which greatly inspired their creativity and enthusiasm. In 2007, China Paper-cuts Museum opened to the public in the back garden of the Wangs' Residence, Yangzhou, greatly promoting the development of Yangzhou paper-cutting.

Features

The subject matter of Yangzhou paper-cutting is quite varied, such as birds, fierce animals, insects, fishes, mountains and grand landscape, and places of historical interest. The images of flowers in four seasons are commonly seen in Yangzhou paper-cuts. In style, some of Yangzhou paper-cuts feature images as a whole and some stress the cutting lines in several styles: thin line paper-cuts; powerful, straight and upright line paper-cuts; soft and curved line paper-cuts. All in all, Yangzhou paper-cutting features exquisiteness, beauty, delicacy and elegance. It shows concretely as follows.

Yangzhou paper-cutting is a beautiful art form with fluid lines. By cutting out pieces of the paper, interior features are formed by making small snips in an area and then cutting away a circle into desired shapes. The main feature of paper-cutting lies in that a continuous line is formed in and around the paper despite numerous small snips.

Yangzhou paper-cutting is refined and exquisite in patterns, for it pays particular attention to a very good combination of images and contents. By cutting and folding, amazing three-dimensional scenes are made out of paper.

Yangzhou paper-cutting has exaggerated and terse images. In handling the images, Yangzhou paper-cutting focuses both on feature extraction and natural continuous lines, which contribute to moderate artistic exaggeration of the whole image.

Yangzhou paper-cutting is in constant pursuit of creative techniques. Many of its characteristics and styles have come into being during the process of technique innovation. In fact, Yangzhou paper-cutting, adopting varied skills, has formed its unique "artistic language".

扬州剪纸有严格的标准，即“方如青砖、圆如秋月、线如胡须、尖如麦芒、缺如锯齿”，只有依照这样的标准，剪出的作品才具备细腻、典雅、剔透的风格。

剪纸大师及其作品

扬州剪纸艺术大师以张永寿为杰出代表。1905年，张永寿出生在扬州一个剪纸世家，是“张氏剪纸”的第五代传人。他天资聪慧，从12岁起随父学艺，经历了70多个艺术春秋，其剪纸从实用性的花样转入富有装饰性的主题性艺术创作，作品呈现出自然流畅、玲珑细致、幽雅清新的特点，是中国南派剪纸的代表。1979年，张永寿被国家授予中国工艺美术大师称号。他一生创作了数千幅作品，其中《百花齐放》、《百菊图》、《百蝶恋花图》等艺术价值极高，被人们称为“剪纸艺术中的观止之作”。

· 张永寿剪纸

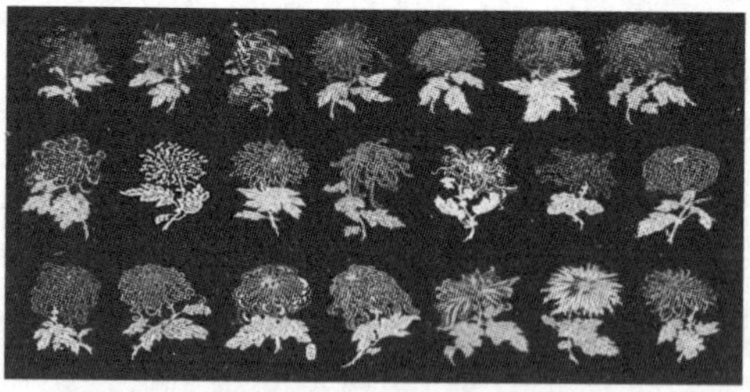

· 张永寿 · 《百菊图》(部分)

1979年，张永寿用了半年的时间创作了《百菊图》剪纸。《百菊图》从整体来看，是一部集剪菊之大全的画卷，每一幅构图，都疏密相间，繁中有简，静中有动，虚实相生。从单幅作品来看，101幅菊花，千姿百态，争奇斗艳，有的柔媚妖娆，有的刚健挺拔，有的似秋荷出水，有的如寒梅傲雪。

1980年，张永寿和他的徒弟们共同创作了《百蝶恋花图》，百花迎百蝶，百蝶恋百花。他剪下的蝴蝶，百般姿态，飞舞花前；他剪下的花枝，娇颜秀色，蹁跹起舞，羞情迎蝶，吐露芬芳。《百蝶恋花图》在日本展出时，被称为“最高之神技”。

There exist strict criteria for making a piece of Yangzhou paper-cut. When you cut it a square, it should be square like a brick; when you cut it round, it should be a perfect arc; when you cut a line, it should be as thin as a hair; if there is an angle, it should be cut sharp; when there is a nick, it should be cut like sawtooth. These are the keys to make exquisite and elegant Yangzhou paper-cuts.

A Great Paper-cutting Master and His Works

Zhang Yongshou was the most outstanding representative among many artists of Yangzhou paper-cutting. Born in 1905 from a paper-cutting family, Zhang Yongshou was the fifth-generation descendant of Yangzhou's Magic Scissors Zhang. He was smart and learned this craftsmanship from his father from the age of twelve. After 70 years' of artistic creation, he changed his theme from practical to ornamental. His works were characterized with natural and flowing beauty, fineness, exquisiteness, freshness and delicacy, making him one of the representatives of the southern style in paper-cutting. In 1979, Zhang Yongshou was titled Master of Arts and Crafts in China. Throughout his lifetime, he produced thousands of paper-cuts, of which the most renowned are All the Flowers Blossoming, One Hundred Chrysanthemums, and One Hundred Butterflies with Gorgeous Flowers.

In 1979, Zhang Yongshou spent half a year creating One Hundred Chrysanthemums. When appreciated as a whole, it looks like a scroll of chrysanthemums in different shapes, styles and movements. Each paper-cut chrysanthemum vividly displays the balanced combination of sparse and dense patterns, complexity and simplicity, emptiness and substantiality, movement and stillness. When appreciated as an individual, the one hundred and one chrysanthemum paper-cuts are so well-refined that they appear to be competing with each other for glamour. Some look enchanting; some stand tall, straight and energetic; some are in full bloom like lotus flowers in autumn; some are blossoming like plum trees braving the snow.

In 1980, Zhang Yongshou and his students together created One Hundred Butterflies with Gorgeous Flowers, in which one hundred gorgeous flowers are greeting one hundred butterflies, and the latter are deeply attached to the former. His paper-cut butterflies take on subtle and different shapes, fluttering up and down in front of the flowers. His paper-cut flowers are blossoming, charmingly and fragrantly, greeting the butterflies shyly. When this masterpiece was on display in Japan, the Japanese praised it as "the top magic on the earth".

·张永寿·《百蝶恋花图》（部分）

·张慕莉·《百子图之一》

张永寿1989年去世后，他的侄女张秀芳、女儿张慕莉传承了他的技艺，并相继获得了江苏工艺美术大师的称号。她们的作品，既有先师遗风，又有自己的创新，美轮美奂，韵味悠长。

·张秀芳·《花鸟四条屏》

After Zhang Yongshou passed away in 1989, his niece Zhang Xiufang and his daughter Zhang Muli have continued his paper-cutting tradition, and have successively won the title Master of Arts and Crafts in Jiangsu. Their works blend the charm of their teacher's brilliant techniques and their own creativity, bringing about surprising loveliness and lingering radiance.